Sons of intimacy

THE GENERATION OF THOSE WHO WILL MANIFEST GOD ON EARTH

MARIANO SENNEWALD

Sennewald, Mariano

Sons and daughters of intimacy : the generation of those who will manifest God on earth / Mariano Sennewald. - 2a ed - Tristán Suárez : Mariano Gastón Sennewald, 2024.

252p. ; 22 x 14 cm.

Translation: Adriana Coppola

 ISBN 978-631-00-2674-9

1. Christian Devotion. 2. Christian Life. 3. Spiritual Growth. I. Title

CDD 248.4 Sennewald, Mariano

Graphic design by Florencia Cáceres

Design by Lic. Marian Quisle

Distribution and sales: editorial@misioninstituto.com

CONTENTS

RECOMMENDATIONS FOR
SONS AND DAUGHTERS OF INTIMACY

It is amazing to see how God is raising and moving the waters of a passionate generation who want to see God as their Lord, longing to see Him manifest as King, but above all they are pursuing God as a Father. This is where the cry of the *Sons and Daughters of Intimacy* begins. I encourage you to humbly present yourself before Him with the highest title that was bestowed over you on this earth, which is to be a child of God, and become truly intimate with Him. I hope this book will take you closer and closer to the heart of the Father as it did with me.

Lucas Conslié
Worship Leader, Toma Tu Lugar Ministries, Córdoba, Argentina

Today in our turbulent world, while some are praying for God to get us out of this so lost planet, and while others are declaring God's judgment, I hear the voice of the Father through Isaiah 60:1-2 proclaiming:

"Arise, shine, for your light has come, and the glory of the Lord rises upon you. See, darkness covers the earth and thick darkness is over the peoples, but the Lord rises upon you and His glory appears over you" (NIV). The problem is not the enemy, the problem is that we don't know who we are. We were designed to glow in the dark, not to run away from it. All creation awaits for the manifestation of the children of God. Mariano's head is resting on the chest of Jesus and he is listening to what the Spirit is saying to the Church: Jesus came to save what was lost.

Our identity is to be *Sons and Daughters of Intimacy.*

Roger Cunningham
Pastor, Iglesia Cristiana La Viña Las Condes, Santiago, Chile

I've had the honor of knowing Mariano Sennewald for some years, I know his family and I can tell about the great work he and the saints of MiSion are developing to further this and the future generations.

I acknowledge him as a true child of intimacy, whom God has given a voice that now comes to us in written form. Undoubtedly, you'll find here years of experience along with present truths which are part of the preparation of the Body of Christ. I fully recommend this book to all those who understand that, as a generation, we are being trained in the secret place to manifest ourselves in public as *Sons and Daughters of Intimacy* with the Father. Thank you, Mariano, for being an instrument of justice in our generation and for offering your life to serve the Church in all the earth.

Gustavo Lara
Apostle, UNGE Ministries, Buenos Aires, Argentina

Unquestionably the coming of Jesus is closer and the Father is restoring the identity of the worldwide Body of Christ. He's doing it through a generation of intimates who are completely free and transformed. They have understood that the major success and purpose of our existence is to fulfill the first and second commandments from the eternal foundation of the heritage of our identity as God's Children, Bride, Kings, and Priests. In my opinion, Mariano Sennewald, besides being a model and sensible prototype for the Sons and Daughters of Intimacy, he is a true precursor, representative, and spokesman of this generation, which will take this message to all the world.

David Lugo
Worship Leader, United States

Every time I've seen Mariano speaking at conferences, I've been dazzled at how he accomplishes and shares something new and provocative with freshness. Through the reading of this book, I realize that he's managed to do the same thing in it. It transmits a high level of energy and enthusiasm about our identity as *Sons and Daughters of Intimacy*. This book has challenged me to see myself as I'm seen in the Presence of God, and to question myself about the gap in between. If you want to take a quantum leap in your spiritual life, read this book.

Gonzalo Zubieta
International Strategy and Leadership Consultant, Santiago, Chile

I believe, without any fear of contradiction, that this book you have in your hands is one of the clearest messages Heaven is speaking to this generation. Not only is it a good book, but it's also an activator; no reader will remain the same after being exposed to the Word of God revealed on every page. When you finish the reading, you'll long to respond to that call, moving from theory to practice, and being part of the representatives and ambassadors of God for this time. Moreover, what blesses me the most is that the author, my friend Mariano, lives what he writes.

Menny Escobar
Pastor, México

The life and message of the Spirit in Mariano Sennewald's voice echo in our being, nourish the eternal, and produce fruit. The book you have in your hands is the result of a life in the secret place, it's the outcome of radical decisions and prophetic times listening to theFather's heart. They are not words thrown to the wind; it's a m essage addressed to a generation who is growing and managing life from the secret and intimate place. This is not a book on arguments nor an exposure of ideas, but a prophetic call to the generations and an apostolic key to the saints. This message will fuel the development of God's designs in your life and it will offer principles of wisdom and divine power to walk in the ways of the Son, to be moved by the Holy Spirit, and to please the Father in everything.

Rodrigo Gorjón
Pastor, Centro Familiar de Adoración, Córdoba, Argentina.

I've been blessed to know my brother Mariano throughout his whole life, and I've witnessed his tireless search for the Presence of God. It is there where he receives the constant revelation upon which his life, family, and ministry are based on. *Sons and Daughters of Intimacy* is God's call to connect yourself to a lifestyle of dependency, abandonment, and leading of the Holy Spirit of God that will transform you to be the exact representation of Jesus and to manifest His glory to this lost world. We will never be able to go in search of the lost without the revelation of first having been found.

Sebastián Sennewald
Evangelist, Iglesia El Encuentro, EMUBA Ministries,
Buenos Aires, Argentina

I know the author of this book more than anyone else. He's been my friend, my fiancé, and now, for many years, we've had a happy marriage. There's something that always moved me and it hasn't changed, but grows stronger every day: his love and untiring desire to hear the Father's voice and make that voice to be heard all around the world. I can clearly see the Father in his life, and this book is only a written sample of what he lives every day. I was the first person who read *Sons and Daughters of Intimacy*, and I'm convinced that it will begin a process of transformation, healing, and restoration to everyone who reads it. In these pages you will be able to discover the Father who dreamed of you, who formed you to be close to Him, and to reveal Him to others. It's my desire that this living message will cause you to fall in love with Jesus, that it will stoke your life as it did–and continues to doing–with me.

Analía Mora de Sennewald
MiSion Ministerial Training Center, Buenos Aires, Argentina

DEDICATION

I dedicate this book to those who have shown me throughout my life the nature of the Father through their lives as children of God. Every small act of divine love that I have seen through hundreds of men and women living as *Sons and Daughters of Intimacy*, has revealed to me that He is real and close; they have increased my desire to live for Him.

To the children of the Wind who are invisibly, anonymously, spontaneously, unpredictably, powerfully, and constantly revealing the Father every week in every corner of the earth, and who are not waiting for the applause of man but for the reward of Heaven.

To those who are willing to die to human and religious traditions in order to establish the Heavenly denomination in this earth.

To those who pay the price of mentoring others rather than just performing tasks, becoming spiritual parents to a generation with an orphan soul.

To those who are giving their lives to transform reality with their eyes fixed on eternity.

ACKNOWLEDGMENTS

To the One who revealed Himself to my life as a close Father, who constantly tells me that *He loves and likes me.* Thank you for being more real than the air I breathe, and for making everything have meaning!

To my perfect mate, the love of my life. Without you, I could never have written this book, you make me feel whole and happy, you're the visible and tangible sign that God rewards those who honor Him.

To the biggest inspiration for this book, my princess: Conie. Everything that's written here was born with you. You have been my major seminary, you gave me a doctorate in love, happiness, and fulfillment, and you've challenged me to be a better man, the dad you deserve. My life was changed when you said "Dad" to me for the first time.

To my parents, I owe you both everything I am. Dad, you're the person who has most influenced my life, I admire you and I'm still learning how the Father is whenever I look to you. Mom, you've always believed in me even when I didn't, I'm the fruit of your prayers and perseverance, thank you for never giving up on me. My brother Sebastián and the rest of my family, thank you for your patience and company in this wonderful adventure.

I especially thank my spiritual children, I have no words to tell you how much I love you. Walking with you, mentoring and enjoying you, has inspired much of the content of this book.

To El Encuentro Church, to the MiSion Institute, and to all my friends of the Kingdom in many cities and nations: What an honor to be part of God's family on earth!

Finally, I want to thank those who made it possible for this message to come to light: Majo Torrez, how can anybody thank such excellence and love? Your designing work is magnificent, but what strikes me most is that you show me Jesus with every attitude, thank you!

Natalia Corsi, you're a blessing for my life, thank you for the dedication to edit the text, your contribution is highly valuable. Gisela Sawin, having your support, advice and collaboration make me grow a lot, thank you. Marianela Liboa, may God reward the time you've spent on corrections, it's a blessing to have you with us. To the whole team of MiSion, this is the fruit of all of us, let's keep striving, for the Father smiles with every step we take.

PROLOGUE

When God created Adam He had the intention of making an extension of His person on earth. The words: image and likeness, in the original refer to shade and shape. We were made in the "form of God" to be His representatives on earth. Satan hates this, because it's a position he will never have again. That's why our enemy, as the father of the rejected, strives to print and burn in people roots of rejection, for humans to feel and live as orphans. However, Christ has come for this, to destroy the works of the devil and to rescue what was lost from Eden: our intimacy with the Father and our identity as children. Jesus will no longer be the only Son of God to become the firstborn of many brothers.

"But as many as received him, to them gave he power to become the sons of God, even to them that believe on his name: Which were born, not of blood, nor of the will of the flesh, nor of the will of man, but of God."
John 1:12-13, KJV

We are children of God by His will and not by our effort of religious practices. This is a result of His intimacy, of having His Spirit, His characteristics, His genetics within us. Today there are many people convinced but only few converts. Conversion is an essential part of the reform God is carrying out by means of His Church in the nations, and that's truly about going back to be like the Father. The evidence that someone is a "son or daughter of intimacy" is not just attending church, singing beautiful songs, or listening to sermons; it's not leaving behind vices or the old way of speech. That evidence must be the character of Christ shown in your life, being a child just like the Father from the inside out. And this we cannot fake or pretend, we must be born again.

We realize that the Holy Spirit is restoring certain truth whenever a revelation is intensified and repeated in different places and in different ways at the same time. In this season, God is talking to us about intimacy and fatherhood as He never has before. For this reason, the book you have in your hands is a tool aligned to the "today" of God for your life, and it will affect your legacy on this earth.

Mariano Sennewald has been my personal friend for many years. I know his heart, his family, and his passion for the authenticity of God. He's certainly the right person to inspire this generation to live as *Sons and Daughters of Intimacy*. When you start reading these pages with expectation to know more about the essence of God, the Holy Spirit will surely bring you out of the superficial and get you into His depths.

However, as it is written:

> *"«What no eye has seen, what no ear has heard, and*
> *what no human mind has conceived»—the things God*
> *has prepared for those who love him—these are the*

things God has revealed to us by his Spirit. The Spirit searches all things, even the deep things of God. For who knows a person's thoughts except their own spirit within them? In the same way no one knows the thoughts of God except the Spirit of God."

1 Corinthians 2:9-11, NIV

By understanding the word *filiation*, I grasped more understanding of the purpose of God in relation to the children born of intimacy. *Filiation* is a word generally used in the legal field to determine that a person is legally a child of his parents. However, in the Latin countries, it is also a term used for companies or any business in determining their extensions or *filiales* (subsidiaries). They are usually attached as close and as similar as possible to the original, which express well what they want to sell or communicate. A clear example of this is McDonald's. One day we had to go with my team to Portugal and it was a fairly long trip with several stops. In nearly twenty-four hours we ate three times in this fast-food chain. It was not that we're fans of that place but it was the only one that was open, and it was also the most "safe" food we had to choose. The advantage is that this burger chain is exactly the same everywhere all over the world (and it has saved us several times). They work with the system of *filiales* (subsidiaries) where all restaurants have to be as similar to the original as possible, and for that reason they are so successful globally. God thought of us so that we could be much more than "fast-food," He created us with the idea that we would be His *filiales*, that is, His children on this earth. The work of Christ on the cross allows us to go back to that former mold and to be in His image and likeness again so that we can represent exactly our Creator, as close to the original as possible.

It would be good for you to take these next few days to rethink if you're really being "a good *filial* (subsidiary)" of Heaven on earth.

Check out if all your fruits, your deeds, your character, and your reactions are showing that you are true son or daughter of intimacy.

I encourage you to be part of the remnant that God has adopted to mark this generation, to do on earth as it is in Heaven. Do not be distracted, because time and chance happen to them all, so take your time and grasp your chance to live like a child of intimacy with God.

Marcos Brunet
Worship Leader, Toma Tu Lugar Ministries, Córdoba, Argentina

INTRODUCTION

The pastor said that God rejoices over us with singing, quoting the prophet Zephaniah. Instantly, one of the ministers began singing from God:

> *My joy is you, son of my heart;*
> *my delight is in you, son of my intimacy.*

In that moment I could feel a warmth in my heart like that of a log fire. That fire began to melt my fears until they were consumed completely. How wonderful it is to hear the music behind the music, and then hear the voice of God wrapped in those words.

A person is not truly free until he hears the voice of the Father whispering his name. I will never understand how God chooses the right time to visit us and revive us. The road to Damascus... Fleeing from Egypt... In prison in Patmos... Sleeping on a stone-pillow..., it seems like deserts are the preferred scenarios for God to speak to His children. Divine love will surely get through any barrier in order to awaken the purpose on those who were chosen from eternity. God is looking for worshipers who worship the Father, and He'll do even the impossible to find them. These true worshipers are His sons and daughters. Where there's a child of God, the Heavens open, the Father's voice is heard, and the Spirit descends visibly. Amidst that picture I imagine you with this book in your hands. The song that I heard that day is beginning to sound within you. You are about to be flooded by the Father's love in a supernatural way. His voice will take you and move you to higher ground as it does an eagle with its young.

It takes years for the enemy to corrupt an identity, but it takes only an instant for God to restore it. We all have been defined by the world. Along the way, someone told us who we were and what we should do. We are the result of experiences that have marked us and conducted our walk. But what if you find out that God says something different about you? What if you've lived so far to meet the expectations of man and not those of your Creator? Is what people say about you matching with what the Father feels when He thinks of you?

Jesus asked, *"Who do they say I am?"* The world had defined Him: *"Some say you are John the Baptist, others Elijah, others Jeremiah or one of the prophets."* The opinion of the people was dissonant with what the Father thought of Him. Then, dissatisfied with the response, He launched the question once more. *"Who do you say I am?"*

It is right there that the passionate disciple said, *"You are the Christ, the Son of the living God."* All of a sudden Jesus could hear someone who defined Him attuned to what his Father thought of Him. Heaven and earth agreed and this son of the intimacy with the Father was activated. That same thing will happen in the next few days, the voice of these pages will be aligned with the symphony of Heaven and suddenly the Holy Spirit will begin to dance within you.

The revelation of Jesus leads us to discover who we are. That's what happened with Peter. Note that the rough fisherman had not heard this statement from any preacher nor had he read it in any book.

Undoubtedly the information he had about Jesus was not part of his religious heritage, but it came from his intimacy with the Father. This man was becoming an unshakable foundation for generations, he was born in the intimacy. And then Jesus Himself defined him. He told Peter who he was and what He would do with him. Jesus named him Simon Peter and told him that on that identity He would build the glorious Church that would unleash hell and unbind Heaven on earth. Simon means "he who hears God," and Peter means "rock" or "stone." Then, "he who hears God is a rock," the years will pass through but he'll remain firm, and Jesus will be able to build His kingdom on him. The eternal empire is made up of sons and daughters. God dreams of a family. There cannot be children if there's no Father. If you have no understanding of who your Father is, you'll never walk as His child. God has adopted you as His son or daughter, have you adopted Him as your Father? The revelation you have of Jesus determines your identity. His name is Eternal Father and you are His child for ever and ever.

Jesus is in love with the Church. For generations He has offered His heart, not to a religious institution but to men and women who respond to His love. That passion is not sterile, it bears fruit: sons and daughters. And they're not born of rules, regulations or human principles. You can inherit a religion, a denomination, and even a ministry, but your relationship with God is not written in the will, it has to be developed and cultivated. I want to encourage you to enter in His room. Let's go together to a place where there's no other sound but the voice of God.

During the next few days I challenge you to turn down the volume of everything around you. Enter that room of intimacy where God will tell you the things He can't tell you in public. What illuminates this environment of love is a light of revelation that will let you see Him like never before. You will discover aspects of God that will fervently attract you to Him. You will also see your naked heart, without the garb of religion. In His mirror, you'll identify areas that urgently need to be healed within you. You will enjoy the aroma of the knowledge of Christ that will perfume the atmosphere and you'll be impregnated of Him to manifest Him everywhere. You'll be embraced, defined, and sent. You have never felt a love like this, no one has looked at you that way. You will enter alone, you'll experience the Father's bosom, and then you'll go forth as part of an army that will manifest God on earth. There is a generation that's about to be born. They will not be born out of a religious system. They are not the result of human effort. They are born in the secret place. These revolutionaries will be birthed in spiritual mangers. Deserts, rooms, trains, buses, playgrounds, parks, beaches, and kitchens will be the delivery rooms where God will enlighten hundreds who will manifest the essence of the not-created One's heart to the mankind. They cannot be found in the crowd, they are lost in the Father's business. They are the heirs of eternity. They are *Sons and Daughters of Intimacy.*

Mariano Sennewald

CHAPTER 1

· Sons and Daughters of Intimacy ·

*The glory of the Father, is to see
His nature in His children.*

*We have many sons and
daughters of the customs and
religious traditions who need to
be reborn of love.*

*Whenever God puts a concern in
your heart it's because He wants
to give you a revelation.*

CHAPTER 1

· Sons and Daughters of Intimacy ·

The news flooded my life with happiness. It was my birthday. My wife woke me up with a breakfast, a very large banner with many pictures and phrases that were full of love and tenderness. In each one of the images there were little pieces of written text reviewing our adventures, travels from the experiences of our early years of marriage. When I thought that was all, she told me that there was still something else and she handed me an envelope. She said that it was the smallest but also the largest present I would ever receive in my life. When I opened it I found the pregnancy test telling me that we would be parents for the first time. We cried together with joy, embraced and worshiped our God for giving us the largest crown and honor we could receive on earth.

Within a few weeks we went over to perform the first ultrasound. From that very moment my heart was struck by a love that I had never experienced before. The doctor said: "Her size is like a grain of rice." Hearing her tiny heart beating in a continuous and profound way was like a message coming directly from God and telling us how much He loved us. All of a sudden, I remembered David's words: *"Your eyes saw my unformed body; all the days ordained for me were written in your book before one of them came to be."*[1]

I then could understand that since we were the size of a grain of rice we were already seen by the Father. My little girl was capturing all the attention of He who had created her. She was the fruit of my love and intimacy with my wife. It was there when God began to speak to me about this book, about a generation of sons and daughters of intimacy, of the love between Jesus and His Beloved.

That was how we began to experience a revival of love in our hearts. In that context, there was an experience that marked me. As the first few months were passing, everyone wanted to know the sex of our baby. We were anxious at every ultrasound, but we could not see it. In one of the visits to the doctor, I remember we spent a long time with the ultrasound system but we couldn't find it out. The doctor said: "It's very unusual to see a baby with crossed legs all the time, and every opportunity we've tried to see again their little feet are not unlocked." My wife and I started laughing. Why? Because I'm just like that, no matter in what position I've fallen asleep, I always awake with my legs crossed. Even when I'm sitting, I always put one foot over the other (I'm just looking at my feet as I write this book, and I have my legs crossed right now!). When we explained the reason of our laughter to the doctor, he said: "It's just like that, the children carry the nature of their parents." Wow! What a wonderful revelation! A generation of children of intimacy who carry the nature of their Father. That is our essence. The day my eyes saw Conie for the first time and I held her in my arms, my life changed. I saw so much of me in her. I've learned the following principle: The glory of the Father, is to see His nature in His children.

She's not me, she's not her mother, but she carries our essence. And she'll always will. Why? Because she was born of intimacy and love.

Children of Religion or Children of Intimacy

God is giving birth to a generation of those who are children of intimacy. When you know them you cannot identify them with a religious tradition but with the nature of the Father. Remember, the glory of the Father is you being like Him. Today we have hundreds of sons and daughters who are similar to denominations and religious structures, but only a few representing the Heavenly denomination. The earth wants to see a generation of children who express the divine nature in power, character and glory. We need sons and daughters that can say like Jesus: *"He who sees Me sees Him who sent Me."*[2] The creation groans for the revealing of the children of God:

> *"For the earnest expectation of the creation eagerly waits*
> *for the revealing of the sons of God."*
> **Romans 8:19, NKJV**

What a paradox! Today there are more Christians than ever on earth, but not all of them are living as children showing the Father. There are forty-one thousand existing evangelical denominations in the world. In countries such as Brazil or the United States, I have seen three churches in the same block. There are hundreds and thousands of forms of worship. Many kingdoms are being built but not all of them have the DNA of the King. *We have many sons and daughters of the customs and religious traditions who need to be reborn of love.* When I travel through different nations meeting Christians, it's very easy to notice their background. Every child of religion answers to paradigms and *clichés* established by the system. It's like they're wearing a shallow gospel, one that was sold in series, poorly genuine, using very predictable and armed phrases. The first thing they ask me when they meet me is, "You are a pastor from what denomination?" And I don't mean that the denominations are not important, but when they determine our identity instead of the nature of the Father, we're in trouble. Structures are not bad, but they were created to support the buildings and not to limit what the architect wants to build. I did not write this book against denominations, not at all, nor do I want you to leave your church, on the contrary, keep on reading and you will see. In fact, I think you're the tool that God will use to fulfill the change that those around you need. But, I also believe that today the Church needs to redefine its identity, despite the place where God's placed each one of His sons and daughters. We must return to our essence together, and that is, to the bosom of the Father. And together, from that place we are to break down the walls that have separated us for centuries. The Church is God's great idea, and it's born of the eternal love of Jesus for us. Let us read the words of Jesus to the Pharisees, who were sons of religion:

> *"But Jesus knew their thoughts, and said to them: «Every*
> *kingdom divided against itself is brought to desolation,*
> *and every city or house divided against itself will*
> *not stand.»"*
>
> **Matthew 12:25, NKJV**

The world does not want to see religious men who have solutions for all things and who think they can fix everything even if they have to burn in bonfires all those who do not think like them. They just need to experience the love, character, power, and glory of the living God through your touch, your words, your hugs, and actions. They don't want speeches or sermons, they long to see and test

God through our lives. If you want to be one of those who carry the Father's nature and manifest His substance to this world, you need an experience like the one Nicodemus lived.

Born From Above

"Now there was a man of the Pharisees, named Nicodemus, a ruler of the Jews; this man came to Jesus by night and said to Him, «Rabbi, we know that You have come from God as a teacher; for no one can do these signs that You do unless God is with him.» Jesus answered and said to him, «Truly, truly, I say to you, unless one is born again he cannot see the kingdom of God.»"

John 3:1-3, NASB

I want to introduce you to Nicodemus, a son of religion. As a child he observed the teachers of the Law, and he dreamed of someday wearing the ornaments and teaching the religious doctrine to the people. His greatest desire was to get to be part of the Sanhedrin and define the religious leadership of the nation. He prepared himself all his life for this. He paid a high price to achieve it. He became an expert in Jewish doctrine and by this time, he has reached a privileged position in the eyes of the priestly aristocracy of Israel. Many consider him a ruler of the Jews. His advice and wisdom is required by all. However, there is a vacuum within him that theology, or the recognition of the religious system, or even the hierarchy he's got in the denomination cannot fill. He's hungry for something he has never tasted.

Suddenly, he finds a man who brings life to the precepts he's been keeping since the days of his childhood. He had never seen those principles other than on papyri, but now he sees them embodied in a mortal man from Nazareth. Questions flood his mind: "What denomination is this man coming from? Is he a Sadducee, a Pharisee? Did he study in a school of prophets or in a seminary of the Law? Where is his synagogue located and who is his Rabbi?" However, this wise man—who knew the Jewish religion perfectly, with its references, temples and currents—realizes that Jesus did not fit into any of them. He comes to the following conclusion: *"Rabbi, we know that You have come from God... for no one can do these signs that You do."* Jesus' life has no natural nor religious explanation. He doesn't respond to any earthly structure, nor can He be identified with any other teacher in Israel. This man came from the Father. The DNA of Jesus is divine. Everything in Him is an expression of the Kingdom that cannot be divided. The daily acts of His life did not fit into the human equations. There is only one source capable of giving birth to a man like Him: God. This is powerfully catching the attention of Nicodemus. Suddenly, he finds himself facing an unknown but attractive scenario. He has not yet discovered the reason for that capturing his interest at all, but he's willing to find it out, even if he has to risk his own reputation. That night, he goes out in a careful search of Jesus. Nobody has to see him. What would those who give their life to save the holy pharisaical tradition do if they see this leader talking to a young passionate man who's just turned the tables in the temple, accusing the religious system of transforming His Father's house into a den of thieves? To be willing to lose position, reputation and control is the first step for those who long to stop being children of religion in order to be transformed into children of the Spirit. Nicodemus did so.

Jesus quickly took command of the conversation. The Master knows what attracted the religious man to this divine appointment. This man needs to see more than to know. Then he says, *"Truly, truly, I say to you, unless one is born again he cannot see the kingdom of God."* The original word for "again" also means "from above." You must be born from above. John explains it this way:

> *"But as many as received Him, to them He gave the right*
> *to become children of God, to those who believe in His*
> *name: who were born, not of blood, nor of the will of the*
> *flesh, nor of the will of man, but of God."*
>
> **John 1:12-13, NKJV**

We cannot fulfill the purpose of God and see His Kingdom if we don't know who we are and where we belong. I have dedicated my first book, *El jardín de la amistad* [The Garden of Friendship], to describe where we come from and where we go to, a place of intimacy where God is waiting for us every day to reveal His heart. God has put this second book, Sons and Daughters of Intimacy, in my heart to reveal who we are, a generation born "from above," from the Father's heart, the fruit of love between Christ and His Church. We are not born "from the earth." John is saying that "God's children were not fathered by people, they were a desire of the Lord." They are not the result of religious structures, denominations or "super" ministers.

They are children of the secret place. When the Church understands who she is, defined by the Father, she'll reach levels of manifestation of the glory of God that were never seen before. If we don't live the process of dying to religion and be born again and from above, we'll never fully understand the Kingdom of God. I think this describes hundreds of people who are now occupying pews in churches every Sunday. But God is giving birth to a generation of sons and daughters of the living God, who will manifest Heaven on earth and the nature of the Father everywhere. They will unify the Kingdom now divided, they will not only know the principles but also live in the power of the Word. They will be moved by the Holy Spirit and their lives will only be explained by supernatural arguments.

Children of the Spirit

I've learned the potential of asking God questions. Many times we don't get answers because we don't ask the right questions. God has no problem with our questions when our true motivation is to hear His voice and receive His direction. Whenever God puts a concern in your heart it's because He wants to give you a revelation. Nicodemus asked, and in that moment a tremendous portal of revelation opened itself for his life, and for us to enjoy this transformative conversation:

"Nicodemus said to Him, «How can a man be born when he is old? He cannot enter a second time into his mother's womb and be born, can he?» Jesus answered, «Truly, truly, I say to you, unless one is born of water and the Spirit he cannot enter into the kingdom of God. That which is born of the flesh is flesh, and that which is born of the Spirit is spirit.»"
John 3:4-6, NASB

To be born again you have to first die. How much of your humanity must die for you to become a child of the Spirit? How many aspects of your character have always accompanied you and are born of the flesh? How many of your dreams come from below and not from above? When God calls you to kill anything in your life, it's because He wants to bring to light something much more glorious. In this process, Nicodemus was dying, but he was also being born a son of intimacy who would defend Jesus in the Sanhedrin before all the religious men;[3] someone, who along with Joseph of Arimathea, would take the body of Jesus to the glorious tomb.[4] A son of the religion was disappearing and an intimate main-character of the Kingdom of Jesus was about to manifest himself. "Born of water" was a term used by the Jews for natural birth. Jesus was saying that besides the natural birth, there must be a birth conceived by the Holy Spirit. Many "living dead" walk all over the earth today who are born of water but not of the Spirit, and therefore they can't see the Kingdom of God. This happens even within the Church itself. I have no doubt that we are experiencing the beginning of a spiritual awakening that will bring a revolution of light to the nations. For years, God's been calling His people to intimate love. We can see the Beloved of the Lord responding to that attractive invitation in a radical and passionate way. Out of this passion, there will be born a generation of children of intimacy.

When I visit different congregations in various nations, regardless of the denomination they are, I notice there are fewer things separating us, and that God is bringing the same identity, similar desires for the Presence of Jesus, and even forms of worship and prayer to be among the things we have in common. Suddenly, out of the forty-one thousand different ways to live the life of the Kingdom, rather than discussing which one is the best, we begin to understand that there is one way, and that is to be like Jesus, a son "from above" and born of the Spirit. Jesus was clear: *"That which is born of the flesh is flesh, and that which is born of the Spirit is spirit."* Who are we? If we are born of the Spirit, I believe that, like Jesus, we need to start identifying ourselves as "sons and daughters of God." With this identity, we have the responsibility to show the nature of the Father in us to all those who see us. I must say that religiosity will become less attractive to the world, but hundreds of Nicodemuses will stake their reputation and position to find God's children who bear the nature of the Father. My heart rejoices when people see my daughter and tell me, *There's no doubt that she is your daughter, she is so like you.* My desire is that, insofar as she grows she'll become a great woman of God who manifests the nature of the Father in the nations. I don't want people to identify her nationality, or religion, or social and cultural status, but I long for her that being a daughter who shows the Father, she would not be defined by any explanation other than the supernatural.

God put this message in my heart for those Nicodemuses who feel empty because of religiosity and who need a spiritual revolution that will change their lives forever. Also, for those who, like Jesus, will atract their own Nicodemuses who are saying: *I don't understand what you do, but I recognize that you come from the Father, because nobody does what you do.* No matter which group you are in, you're part of a generation that is about to manifest itself on earth as sons and daughters of intimacy. Wherever they are, they'll cause the Heavens to open, the Spirit to descend in a visible way, and the voice of the Father to be heard on earth saying, *These are my beloved children and my heart feels pleasure for them.*

How can this internal change take place? How do I know if I am a child of religion or of the intimacy? How can I be transformed into a protagonist of what God will do on earth in the coming years? These were the questions that led me to give birth to this book. Similar queries were asked to Jesus by the chief of the Pharisees. I encourage you to move forward with me in this wonderful journey and to discover how Jesus transformed Nicodemus into a son of intimacy.

PRACTICAL GUIDE CHAPTER 1

· *Sons and Daughters of Intimacy* ·

Questions to share in groups, cells or leadership teams:

1. What are the characteristics of the Father's nature that must be restored in the children of God?

2. What would happen in the Body of Christ and in the world, if the children of God walked revealing the Father?

3. What symptoms of religiosity do you recognize in the Church today that produce division and prevent the nature of the Father from manifesting?

4. How can we guide others to live as "Sons and Daughters of Intimacy"?

Personal application exercise:

Make a list of practical decisions that you will make in your daily life so that the nature of the Father grows in your life and that when many see you they can see Him.

CHAPTER 2

· Children of the Wind ·

*Without the breath of life,
Adam was inert mud. The body
without the spirit is simply
a piece of flesh. The Church
without the government of the
Spirit is just bricks and people
piled up.*

*God has already taken our
shape through Jesus, so that we
would be able to take His shape
through the Spirit.*

*Jesus does not want to distract
us from the world, He wants to
draw us into the Kingdom.*

CHAPTER 2

· *Children of the Wind* ·

On my first trip to Bolivia I met some extraordinary friends. I identify the night I'm about to describe below as one of the most wonderful nights in my life. The warmth of the pastoral family home where I was staying, could only be achieved if the Presence of God was the very core of that place. It was an evening where the passionate talks and stories of the Kingdom were eclipsing the delicious food that was on the table. The pastors began to describe one of the most difficult and—at the same time—glorious moments of their lives. The story was about their youngest daughter. When she was fourteen years of age, her parents asked her what she wanted to receive for her fifteenth birthday gift. In many Latin American countries, they usually entertain fifteen-year-old girls with a party or a trip to enjoy with her friends or family. The girl's response at first did not seem bizarre. *A journey*, she said. Until that moment, you can imagine the excitement of her parents because of their daughter's choice, they would not have exorbitant costs for meals, drinks, and party favors, but they would enjoy an amazing time with the family instead. *Very good! And where would you like to go?* they asked. *Iran, to smuggle Bibles*, replied the passionate teenager.

I remember how these precious children of God, described that event. All of a sudden, their blood froze inside of them and hundreds of questions filled their minds and even their mouths. *Iran?! The country who is enemy number one of the people of Israel?! The place where if they find someone with a Bible the luckiest thing that person can get is to spend life in prison before being killed or tortured?! What would they do to a little fifteen-year-old girl if they found her with a Bible?* They quickly began to explain all the scenarios why this was crazy and that in no way they'd authorize her to perform such "suicide"—I meant, travel. For about eight months they tried to convince her to change her mind. They used arguments, photos of torture, and real stories of missionaries who are still prisoners in those nations in the Middle East. But, how difficult it is to break the will of someone who has within her the DNA of the One who was able to leave His throne and give His life for others to obtain it! During that time, that girl's parents realized that no reason could make her retreat from this desire, because those who have died to everything because of Jesus, they have nothing to lose, not even their own life. So, after a tough process, the parents of this "daughter of intimacy" heard God telling them that this was His plan and they should allow the trip.

Soon, Cecilia was boarding on this divine adventure. At the airport in Iran, she heard a voice from the Spirit telling her she should enter through a door that had a sign reading: "Diplomats Entry." The young passionate girl obeyed. When they saw her, the immigration police welcomed her and even checked her luggage for her. Amid such supernatural intervention, the Holy Spirit whispered to her again: *Welcome Ambassador of the Unshakable Kingdom.* Within minutes she was in this hostile nation with a suitcase full of Bibles.

Many people received the treasure of the Word of God through this brave warrior.

Weeks later she was reunited with her family to tell them the heavenly experiences she had lived. I have other friends who have introduced Bibles in Iran in miraculous ways. Customs' scanners broke just as they were entering, the policemen at the scanners got itchy eyes when checking their luggage, and similar stories.How I love the life of those people who can only be explained supernaturally! In them I see the Father's nature. I have rarely observed in the eyes of a person as much freedom and love as in my Bolivian friend's eyes. This is one of many examples that could be used to describe the "children of the wind." Those "invisible ones" who are moved by the Spirit, unpredictable for the natural system, but they make themselves felt and everything they touch is healed. God is blowing from His own mouth on these carriers of the breath of life on earth. Jesus referred to them when discussing with Nicodemus:

> *"That which is born of the flesh is flesh, and that which*
> *is born of the Spirit is spirit."*
>
> **John 3:6**

If you look at the commentary in your Bible, you will notice that the same Greek word used in this passage means both spirit and wind. Wind represents a generation of invisible ones, not so interested in being seen, but they do make themselves felt. They cannot be controlled nor trapped in human and religious systems. They are driven and led by the Holy Spirit. There is a dimension of intimacy with God and passion for His Presence in which your spirit and God's are intertwined and you are literally possessed by Him. The Spirit begins to determine your steps, movements, and He begins to see Christ in you, the hope of glory. This is a key feature that differentiates children of the religion from the sons and daughters of intimacy. While the first respond to religious paradigms and their movements are determined by human traditions, the children of the Spirit are literally moved and directed by God.

Invisible and Unpredictable

I would like to return to the story of Jesus and Nicodemus. In this passionate talk, the Lord uses the figure of the wind to describe those born "from above:"

> *"Do not be amazed that I said to you, «You must be born again.» The wind blows where it wishes and you hear the sound of it, but do not know where it comes from and where it is going; so is everyone who is born of the Spirit."*
>
> **John 3:7-8, NASB**

What a wonderful description of the generation God is raising up in the earth! The wind is not seen but heard. So are the children of intimacy. They have a sound. They are not so concerned about the recognition of the system, but they have a prophetic voice that's clear and powerful for these times. I understand that God is releasing a creative anointing upon those willing to live the process of dying to religion and birthing of the Spirit. This voice will be manifested through songs, books, messages, and projects. It will be heard not only in temples but also in universities, businesses, legislative offices, and even presidential palaces. A fresh wind is blowing over the nations. They are the invisible ones, whenever you want to see them you'll only see the Spirit in them.

I would like to make the following exception: when I speak of this generation, I do not mean only young people, it doesn't have to do with the age, but with people who are part of the army that God is recruiting for what's coming. In fact, it's very likely that in this story, Nicodemus was not young, for he was a ruler of the Jews and this hierarchy was granted only to those who had a religious reputation gained through the years. Jesus goes on with the description of the children of the wind saying, *"but do not know where it comes from and where it is going."* The sons and daughters of intimacy are "unpredictable." This is the antithesis of religiosity, which is working hard to make the children of God predictable. Everything has to be controlled and structured. There is no room for surprise. We do not want anything to surprise us, or escape out of our hands, we fail even accepting when God wants to break into our structured services and we often call "disorder" to the unpredictable. I totally agree that we need order, but when in order to achieve it, we take off the "uncontrollable" God from the equation, we lose the most important thing.

Religiosity produces fear of the new. The liturgical programs are increasingly rigid and safe. Nothing can leave what has already been planned. We have services in series, like flawless products for demanding customers. If the time goes on a little longer, consumers would complain and never return next week. We have schedules for worship, for announcements, for the sermon. There's no room for unpredictable events. Everything must come from some place and go to another. That's exactly opposed to what Jesus said. Perhaps it works, but it does not mean it's from the Spirit. The children of the wind are unpredictable. They are guided and moved by God in everything.

I declare that in the coming years, we will know when our services will start, but we'll have no idea when they will end, because the move of the Spirit will be so strong that He will take the control and we'll lose it. We can prepare the altar, summon the people and even the prophets of Baal, but we cannot make the fire. We must develop hearts for attracting the divine glory. When each service is about to start, the children of the wind will ask, *Holy Spirit, what do you want today? We have our plan, but if you don't break in and manifest yourself, nothing will make sense.* When someone would ask us, *How are the services in your denomination, in your church?* We will say: *I truly have no idea, because every week is different, it's never the same, but we always hear and experience the presence of the Living God.* The meeting will not be focused on men but on the beauty of Jesus and the power of God. Sermons will not be what produce miracles, but they will explain and teach about the glory experienced by each one of those reached by the wind of the Spirit through His children. Just as at Pentecost, the fire of the Spirit and the mighty wind will fall first, and then the "Peters" of this generation will explain: *"These men are not drunk, as you suppose... but this is what was spoken of through the prophet Joel..."*[5] God is bringing a change and those who have ears to hear are hearing the sound of the wind. Human control will be transformed into divine fear. Pride into dependence. Sin into holiness. And slavery into freedom.

Moved by the Spirit

The world is changing. The Church is changing as well. Evolution is part of life. Every day we grow. All living people change. We must address these transformations towards the Perfect Man and grow every day to His stature.

We live in a time when we have realized that religiosity is not enough. The Theoretical Gospel has failed. We must return to the point where we turned aside and get back on track. All the changes you're producing in this time should bring you to a life filled and moved by the Holy Spirit. *Without the breath of life, Adam was inert mud. The body without the spirit is simply a piece of flesh. The Church without the government of the Spirit is just bricks and people piled up.* There is a spiritual dimension described in Romans 8 called "Life in the Spirit" (I recommend you read the whole chapter). The summary of this wonderful story about what the children of the Spirit should be is in verse 14:

"For all who are being led by the Spirit of God, these are sons of God."

Romans 8:14, NASB

I want you to notice the relation between being a child of God and being moved by the Spirit. Jesus spoke to Nicodemus about this. Being filled with the Spirit is an experience, being guided and moved by the Spirit is a process, a lifestyle. He not only wants to fill you, He also wants to lead you. He does not want to give you just a glorious service, His commitment is for you to live a glorious life. A son of the wind is driven in his daily walk by the will of the Spirit. I must ask you: "Are you so taken by the Holy Spirit that He guides every step you take? Who rules in your life, the flesh or the Spirit?" When the Spirit guides the life of a person, He constantly leads him to the Father's will. He takes and determines your movements. He bows your actions toward the devotion to God and the extension of His Kingdom. You can no longer move your way because He directs you in everything.

A Glove in the Hands of God

Many years ago, I attended a conference and I remember a message that has marked me. It was on lives controlled by the Spirit. The renowned speaker used the example of a glove. What I remember most in that preaching is this illustration. It was simple and powerful. He said: *We are the gloves, and God is the hand. If He takes us, we can no longer do what we want, He will possess us completely, He will move us and our lives will be controlled by His Spirit.* In my memory of that day, this is the prayer I raised to the Father: "I want to be a glove in your hands." Over the years I discovered that this example had much more spiritual sense than I thought. The glove is shaped by the hand. We have the form of God, we were created according to His image and likeness. Thus, as the glove serves only to the hand, we also were designed to be filled by Him. When God owns us through His Spirit in an absolute way, we take His form. The glove becomes part of the hand, as we become part of God. Paul said: *"It is no longer I who live, but Christ lives in me."*[6] If someone touches us with a glove, we do not attribute the touch to a piece of wool, but to the person. In this spiritual dimension, the children of the wind are gloves in the hands of God. When we touch someone, people do not see us, instead they see the One who has taken us. After a service, people will say: *God spoke to me,* instead of: *What a tremendous preacher.* Others will declare: *I felt the touch of God,* instead of attributing the glory and power to men. God wants us to take His shape and this can only happen when we're taken by the Spirit. God desires to determine our movements. He longs for us to be one with Him. My friend Cecilia was a glove in the hands of God to introduce Bibles in Iran. I have other friends from the United States, pastors who left everything to open a work in Cochabamba (Bolivia) thirty years ago. Today there is a church in that place with an auditorium for over a thousand people, a school for hundreds of children, and an orphanage, and they are impacting more than a city. They are impacting a nation. The day these beloved brothers left everything they became gloves in God's hands to caress that nation. People do not grant the glory to them, they only understand that God moved over there. I have a friend who's working in India, recruiting girls from their families so they will not be given in marriage (in that place they give them to be married as young as five years of age). Many of them die sexually lacerated, or are enslaved all her lives. Parents do this aberration only for a little money. My friend is a glove on the hand of God to embrace these little girls. Another pastor I met in a country closed to the Gospel (I will not mention him for security matters), has been imprisoned for five years for preaching Christ. Recently, in the trial, they told him that if he denied Jesus, they would give him freedom and he'd be able to return to his wife and daughters. He replied, *I can lose my freedom, I can lose my wife, I can lose my daughters, but I cannot lose my faith in He who made me free for eternity, Jesus Christ.* I could enumerate many more cases of invisible ones who—every week in different cities and moved by the Spirit—are building the Kingdom of God and experiencing the supernatural. They have surrendered their will, but they are part of a greater desire. They have decided to live the life of the Spirit and surrender their flesh. They all live in fullness. A friend taught me that fullness is not in having it all, but in having no need of anything. This can only come from the experience of the Spirit filling every space within us. Therefore, in His Presence we have fullness! *God has already taken our shape through Jesus, so that we would be able to take His shape through the Spirit.* As children we have the nature of the Father. The only way to become children of the wind is by stopping the feeding of our flesh in all its forms and begin the nourishing of the spirit. We must kill all carnality in our lives, everything that wants to fill the glove and direct it towards other purposes. I define "carnality" as that what "cools" your fervent longing for God. Worship is a matter of desire. Everything you want more than Jesus is idolatry. In this way, the ministry itself can become an idol if you prefer being used rather than being loved.

The Spirit always creates an appetite within you that can only be supplied by Jesus and His will. All "theology" that obstructs your worship to God and your love to your neighbor is incorrect. Being taken by the Spirit will draw you to Him and will connect you to others. God will lead you to a glorious destiny, and, all of a sudden, you will smile as only those who have attained His fullness do.

Hunger for the Supernatural

A religious person can become a child of the wind when he allows himself to hunger for the supernatural. This is what happened to Nicodemus. It was the inexplicable what attracted him: *"No one can do these signs that You do."* Religion makes you put your eyes on the natural and the explainable. I remember a conversation I had several years ago with a youth leader of a large church in my nation. He said: *I only believe what I understand and I can check, for me the rest is mysticism.* Where do we place faith in that equation? We confuse spirituality with mysticism. We cannot see and experience the Kingdom of God without hunger for the spiritual, because this is its substance. The spiritual is invisible, unpredictable, and—at the same time—powerful, transforming, and attractive. So are the children of the wind. So is Jesus.

Let us return to the story of Nicodemus. After this wonderful description of a child of the Spirit made by Jesus, Nicodemus' head is about to explode (I hope yours, too!). His spirit is about to be moved, actually. So he asks the question:

"Nicodemus said to Him, «How can these things be?»"
John 3:9, NASB

We note that this second question is not as long as the first. Sometimes words are useless for those who are only waiting to see what they never saw. There is a deep desire to live a change, a transformation. His question states that there is hunger for the supernatural in this religious soul. Nicodemus asks the question we all want to ask: *"How can these things be?"* In other words, *How do I stop being religious and be part of this Kingdom that you're describing? How, as a man who fervently defended the Jewish denomination in the Sanhedrin, who has attended the synagogue all my life and taught there, can I enter this spiritual dimension?* I have felt in my spirit the same question in many men and women of God I met. Some express it as a feeling of fear to be missing something. Others know that there is more, but they think they're too old for a change. They prefer the comfort of the known rather than the freshness of what God is sending. I understand that because I was there. On that side, much is known, but we don't see anything of the Kingdom. The temples are full of people who know a lot and see nothing. Jesus is not speaking to Nicodemus about knowing, but about seeing. This makes his heart explode in a short question: *How do I do this?* If the question of this religious man is the same as yours, you need to ask it. It's not enough to think it—it is time to express your hunger. Nicodemus had to leave his comfort "at night" and go in search of his transformation. You must leave your comfort and, in intimacy (at night), start looking for the Spirit as you never did before. That hunger, that passion will take you to the revelation. They will open a door before you to a dimension of the Spirit where you will no longer have the control, everything will be ruled by Him. This is not something you can get from a book, or a man, it's something that only those who dare to cross the line and talk to Him face to face can get. Nicodemus is right there, at the exact moment where his life will take a new direction. He is just about to jump from the comfortable, cushioned seats of religion to the adventure platform of the Kingdom. That's the difference between people like my Bolivian friend and many other teenagers who are entertained every week in our churches with the intention of not going to a nightclub. *Jesus does not want to distract us from the world, He wants to draw us into the Kingdom.* This is what distinguishes those who are living as children of the wind, moved and directed each day to supernatural adventures, from those who are content with a theoretical Christianity, based on laws and knowledge that only cool our love for God and for our neighbor. That is the line that this man is about to cross, and I cry out to God for that to be the same border you're about to pass. Are you ready?

PRACTICAL GUIDE CHAPTER 2

· *Children of the Wind* ·

Questions to share in groups, cells or leadership teams:

1. Let's cite a moment in our lives when God took control and directed us to do something unpredictable. What consequences were there?

2. Seeking to keep the biblical order and vision of the ministry to which we belong, how could we provoke moments when the Holy Spirit takes control and guides us to experience the manifest glory of God?

3. What are the obstacles that prevent the supernatural from manifesting in our midst?

4. What concrete actions can we take to grow our hunger for the manifestation of the Presence of God?

Personal application exercise:

What areas of your life do you need to surrender to the Holy Spirit to become a glove in His hands? Make a list of those areas, and in the second column write a practical decision you will make to achieve them.

AREA	PRACTICAL ACTION

CHAPTER 3

· Eyes Fixed on the Father ·

A divine word sustains what circumstances weaken.

There may be theology, law, reputation, but when there is no intimacy there is discouragement.

Every crisis breaks out when we remove our eyes from Christ.

CHAPTER 3

· *Eyes Fixed on the Father* ·

A week after Conie was born, we lived perhaps one of the most difficult moments of our lives. She was diagnosed with an infection that was making her lose weight at an alarming rate. She was born with almost 6.6 lb. But in a few days she was barely over 5 lb. We had to take her for emergency hospitalization. I remember we came to the clinic a few days before when we had lived moments of full joy, but now the picture was totally opposite. It was a very cold winter day, and the fear for our daughter made it look frozen and dark (so I remember it). The place was crowded, people were literally packed in the hallways because they were short staffed. We were treated in the emergency room. When they examined her and saw the doctor's order, the faces of the doctors were reflecting the seriousness of the matter. They told us to wait. After a while, the head of neonatology approached and, with a worried face, told us that the clinic was at capacity, no more babies were coming in the sector intended for intensive care of newborns, and Conie would be moved to another clinic. I couldn't even move her from that place on my own, because her life was in danger. We had to wait for an ambulance equipped for the situation. In other words, they could not receive her and I could not take her with me. I was in the middle and couldn't do anything. We were placed in an inner hallway and they said they had urgently requested a transfer, but because many clinics were in the same condition, the situation was complex and they had to wait for answers. We waited six unending hours in that narrow, dark hallway. I will never forget that feeling. My wife was crying, my daughter, too. No one had told me how to act in such a situation. I had only seven days to learn to be a father, I felt completely helpless and vulnerable. I did not understand how God had given me something so wonderful, and now maybe He'd ask for it back.

In the middle of this situation, I lived my own process with the Father. I remembered that a few months before Conie's delivery, a three-year-old girl from our church, had awakened telling her parents this: "Conie will be safe and sound." She repeated that all day long. Her dad had called me amazed at the time. He said, "Mariano, she never speaks like that, I don't know why she says this, but she is saying that your daughter will be safe and sound." In the middle of that hallway, I remembered those words. If God had awakened the spirit of a girl to prophesy this things a few months before, what could be out of His control? While everything in the natural was saying one thing to us, the Spirit began to whisper another. Within this scenario, one of my disciples sent me a song she had just composed. The lyrics said: "I'm here Dad, looking into your eyes... And I see in You, that everything is under your will, I will fear no thing, You take care of me, Mighty God, Admirable, Eternal Father it's You..." I fixed my eyes on the Father, and fear began to dissipate. I strengthened myself in the Lord, and full of confidence I hugged my wife, I spoke these words to her and we worshiped Jesus. For the next month, all the tests seemed to have adverse medical outcomes. But we had one word: "Conie will be safe and sound." When a word comes from God, no matter through the mouth of who it is expressed, it's powerful enough to twist any prognosis. We had the diagnosis of earth and of Heaven. We decided to hold the clinic of Jehovah *Rapha*, He who heals everything. Finally, the report of the earth had to bow to the one of Heaven. Conie was discharged, and she increased her weight to such point that the doctors, who knew of our faith, told us: "Ask your people to stop praying because she is going now to the other extreme!"

I've learned many principles in that process and I want to share some of them with you. The first one is that every crisis begins when we take off our eyes from Jesus and put them on the circumstances. No matter how great the storm may be, if Jesus is resting, I can rest. I've also learned that God prepares us for every adversity. He does not allow us to go through anything without placing within us the resources to overcome it. That word from this beautiful girl, which at first we took as something very cute but without much understanding, became the anchor that kept the boat steady in the midst of the storm. *A divine word sustains what circumstances weaken.* Another lesson I've learned is that your trust in God in the middle of trials will be your major worship. Feeling the gaze of the Father fixed upon us is enough to make a trembling heart find peace.

The early months of Conie's life were a great seminar for me. I learned aspects of the Father as I never had before. At first, due to medicines and treatments, she cried so much. I used to stare at her and say, *Don't cry, my little girl, Daddy is here with you.* She didn't have the ability to set her eyes on me, she looked all around and wept. At some point, she could look at me and found my loving eyes captivated by her. Despite how strong her crying was, when she looked at me, she smiled. Then I understood that our worship is a response to the loving gaze of the Father. If worship is our smile to Him, it can only manifest itself when we find His eyes upon us. Our soul cries when we can't find His attention. We are like that baby who has a couple of very large eyes before her, but her crying doesn't allow her to see them. Fixing our eyes on Jesus sets the channel through which our soul is strengthened and our spirit is nourished. That is the link that triggers the sincerest worship and attracts the favor from Heaven into our lives. Faith's eyes awaken you to the reality that He is in front of you and He loves you so much that He just can't take His eyes away from you. I remember, in this testing process, when they injected vaccines into my daughter's small thigh. My heart was torn when she burst into tears. I stared at her, and said: *Although you don't understand what's going on, this pain is for your own good. It will hurt a bit now, but it will make you stronger later. In the midst of your pain, Daddy is with you, look at me my daughter, and find my eyes fixed on you.* Our heavenly Father is like that. All the pain He allows sometimes in our lives is to strengthen us, and not for bad. From time to time we need thesedoses of testing, in order to experience a complete healing. Seeing the Father smiling when He is looking at us makes us stronger. Maybe if I put it this way it would sound more familiar: *"For the joy of the Lord is your strength."[7]* More than once the eyes of religion will tell you it's not from God. Instead of a glance of love, you will find a look of judgment. Your own flesh will join forces with the accuser, and raise your own finger to increase the crisis. The enemy will propose other options for you to look at such as fixing your sight on men. And many times you will think that if you don't receive the help of a person, you would not leave the pit. That will make you more dependent on others rather than God, and without noticing, it will lead you to idolatry. Sometimes he'll whisper in your ear that your situation is because of someone else's guilt. He often acts by blaming your authorities (the devil has always had a serious problem with authority). You will find yourself blaming your parents, your pastors or someone else. But, if you get through those walls and fix your eyes on Jesus, you will find the greatest, tender glance of love cheering you up. You will know you're not alone, you were just looking at the wrong place, like a baby who is distracted by everything and cries. His eyes will captivate you, and you will hear His voice saying: *I have not left you. This process is necessary, look at me alone and you will find the place of your security.* Then you'll smile.

The Power of Looking to Jesus

Let us look at the following story in Numbers 21:4-9, which has a great connection to what we have seen so far:

> *"Then they journeyed from Mount Hor by the Way*
> *of the Red Sea, to go around the land of Edom; **and***
> ***the soul of the people became very discouraged***
> ***on the way.** And the people spoke against God and*
> *against Moses: «Why have you brought us up out of*
> *Egypt to die in the wilderness? For there is no food*
> *and no water, and our soul loathes this worthless*
> *bread.» **So the Lord sent fiery serpents among the***
> ***people, and they bit the people; and many of the***
> ***people of Israel died.** Therefore the people came to*
> *Moses, and said, «We have sinned, for we have spoken*
> *against the Lord and against you; pray to the Lord*
> *that He take away the serpents from us.» So Moses*

> *prayed for the people. Then the Lord said to Moses,*
> *«**Make a fiery serpent, and set it on a pole; and***
> ***it shall be that everyone who is bitten, when he***
> ***looks at it, shall live.**»"*
>
> **Numbers 21:4-9, NKJV**
> Emphasis added by the author

This is a wonderful story. The people of Israel are in the "middle" land. It's been a while since they have left Egypt but, it looks like the Promised Land is never getting closer. The "middle" land is a very difficult place to be in the road for a Christian. It's where you are tested to find out if you're a son of the Spirit or a son of religion. It is a hostile, barren, and dry place. There does not seem to be a lot of bread and water, and soul is annoyed by reality. The wilderness can be the scene of your maximum encounters with God, or it can be the cemetery where your soul will bury your whole being. If, at that point of your process, you remove your eyes from Jesus to put them elsewhere, you will probably waste away your strength and you'll stay apart from the promises. Passing a test involves not taking your eyes from God even in the midst of pain. This makes you stronger. Placing your eyes on men or on circumstances when you go through the "middle" land can be fatal. This is where discouragement is brewing. Then we read the following sentence: *"The people became very discouraged"* Being discouraged means being without the breath of God, it means having the Spirit quenched.[8] Discouragement is a fruit of a stifled Spirit. *"For God did not give us a spirit of cowardice, but rather a spirit of power and of love and of self-discipline"* (2 Timothy 1:7, NRSV). The discouragement God's people are experiencing in this verse is related directly to their weak communion with Him. *There may be theology, law, reputation, but when there is no intimacy there is discouragement.* For this reason, the children of the wind cannot walk in discouragement, because this courage is their essence. Whenever discouragement knocks on the door of their lives, they find the strength in the Spirit of God, raising their eyes to the Father.

The next step these sons of religion take in the desert is looking for who is responsible. Encouraged by one who has always had serious problems retaining their authorities, they blame God and Moses. Have you noticed the sequence? First, they quenched the Spirit, then they got angry with their pastor. Instead of taking responsibility for your own situation, the religious spirit will always propose you someone else to blame. Raising our soul against the authorities God has established is a non-negotiable issue for Him. It was that same sin the one the kingdom of darkness was founded on. Questioning the authority did not exist until the devil did it. God is radical about this aspect all over the Bible. Following these steps of discouragement (losing communion with God) and of criticizing (projecting our mistakes in others), there is the consequence—the fiery serpents bringing death among the people of God. As we see, it's the same way Satan works today. The attitudes that are wrong to the divine nature open the doors of our gardens for snakes to keep entering. It happened to Adam, it happened to the people here in this story, and it happens to many Christians today. These are clear symptoms of children of religion. They are like gloves filled with many things but the Spirit of God.

After this terrible situation the people repent. We can see that the pain strengthens some of the surviving ones. Their hearts turn to God, they run to Moses, and cry for mercy. A repentant heart is irresistible to God. This cry comes to the Father and He sends a response. Perhaps, for us, the sensible solution would be to remove all the fiery serpents. But the logic of God surpasses all understanding. He does not take away the snakes, but He asks Moses to make a bronze serpent, to put it on a pole and lift it up. Every Israelite who looks upon this divine provision, will be redeemed from death. Note the detail: God tells Moses that salvation will come through a specimen of the same species which brought the curse, but this one, sanctified, will shine in a different way, and those who look at it will be restored. Does this sound familiar? Of course, it represents Jesus. The last Adam, one of the same species as the one who introduced the curse in the world. But this sanctified man, the Son of God, will remove the condemnation and judgment of those who look at Him. And, what is the secret of those who are released from snake venom? It's fixing their eyes on Him. God does not automatically remove the curse of the world, but He teaches the children of Israel to worship. He provides a path of redemption. That path is a person, a man: Jesus. As we learned from the story of the beginning, to look is to worship. We are transformed into what we look at. When our gaze meets His, there is joy, restoration, and freedom. Jesus says to every disciple: *Follow me!* In order to follow someone, we cannot lose sight of him. We can't follow Jesus if we are distracted with the world, or with circumstances. The Pharisees were discussing doctrine in sterile enclosures, while the disciples were following Jesus and participating in supernatural works. What are your eyes on? In the glorified Jesus, we find the breath that is needed in the "middle" land. The logic of religion breaks down before the power of the risen Christ. The fiery serpents may remain in the world, but they no longer have power. They remind us that if we don't look at the bronze serpent, we'll die. Jesus says:

> *"These things I have spoken to you, so that in Me you*
> *may have peace. In the world you have tribulation, but*
> *take courage; I have overcome the world."*
> **John 16:33, NASB**

The bronze serpent represents Jesus. In a moment, I will show this from the very mouth of Jesus Himself. Everyone who has access to it can be free. We are not transformed "doing tasks" or "singing songs" but "watching" His glory.[9] And note the tense, it is present continuous. It's the permanent action of having our eyes fixed on Him. David managed to have a heart after God's heart because he had discovered this secret:

> *"My eyes are ever toward the Lord, for He shall pluck my feet out of the net."*
> **Psalm 25:15, NKJV**

> *"They looked to Him and were radiant, and their faces were not ashamed."*
> **Psalm 34:5, NKJV**

Let's leave the story of Moses and return to our scene between Jesus and Nicodemus. Jesus has described, so far, the children of the Spirit as children of the wind, invisible, unpredictable, and supernatural. Nicodemus is desperate to get into this dimension, and he asks Jesus how he could manage to be a son of the wind. Are you ready to know Jesus' answer?

Going From a Religious to a Son or Daughter of Intimacy

> *"Jesus answered and said to him, «Are you the teacher of Israel, and do not know these things? Most assuredly, I say to you, We speak what We know and testify what We have seen, and you do not receive Our witness. If I have told you earthly things and you do not believe, how will you believe*

> *if I tell you heavenly things? No one has ascended*
> *to heaven but He who came down from heaven, that*
> *is, the Son of Man who is in heaven. And as Moses*
> *lifted up the serpent in the wilderness, even so must*
> *the Son of Man be lifted up, that whoever believes in*
> *Him should not perish but have eternal life.»"*
>
> **John 3:10-15, NKJV**
> Emphasis added by the author

Jesus' answer is blunt and clear. The only one who can speak about the Heavenly name is He who knows it and saw it. That means that our eyes are to be set on the One who came down from Heaven, the Son of Man. He is "*In whom are hidden all the treasures of wisdom and knowledge.*"[10] Jesus is calling here a person—who for years has laid his eyes on the Law, on ministers, on men, and on denominational systems—to fix his eyes on Him. Jesus is aware that this man knows the Law and that he certainly has in his bedroom a large "poster" of Moses, as all major Pharisees have. Nicodemus has already read and studied hundreds of times the history of the fiery serpents and bronze serpent. He loves this story and he knows all the details. He has taught that same story from several platforms. And suddenly, Jesus is saying that the serpent represents Him Himself. "*And as Moses lifted up the serpent in the wilderness, even so must the Son of Man be lifted up, that whoever believes in Him should not perish but have eternal life.*" Can you imagine the impact on the spirit of Nicodemus? *How can this be? Are You the provision from Heaven to bring freedom to a people discouraged and attacked by the enemy?* The scales fall down from the eyes of this child of religion, and he realizes he must count everything as rubbish in order to know Him who is now before him. Just as it happened with Paul, hundreds of Pharisees and teachers of the Law, since the first day they looked at Jesus with revelation, they could never stop looking at Him. Only those who stare at Him are transformed from glory to glory in His own image. *Looking* at someone and *fixing* our eyes on that person are not the same. When I was a single man I had looked at other girls, until one day my eyes were fixed on her who is my wife today, and I could never stop looking at her. Jesus is saying to Nicodemus: *If you want to enter this heavenly realm, I am the door. From now on you you'll have to look at me, and follow me. The Father will lift me up, and everyone who looks at me will be transformed.* The Gospel is not a philosophy of life; it is a person: Jesus. Without Him, there is no Gospel. The Master did not say to His disciples, *From now on you'll have to schedule a time slot for Me on Sundays.* He did say, *"Follow me."* The Gospel is not attending a worship meeting, but following a Person. And to follow someone, we should not lose sight of Him. Could it be that among so, many strategies, activities, and ministries we have lost sight of Jesus? I think so, and this has made us to have hundreds of children of religion and very few children of the wind today. But Jesus continues to recruit disciples in this generation, and He is saying to them, *"Follow me."* I think that is the message Jesus is shouting out loud through this book.

Let Us Fix Our Eyes on Jesus

"Looking unto Jesus, the author and finisher of our faith,
who for the joy that was set before Him endured the cross, despising
the shame, and has sat down at the right hand of the throne of God."

Hebrews 12:2, NKJV
Emphasis added by the author

It's time to fix our eyes on Him, for His eyes are fixed on you.[11] If you look at men, or circumstances, you'll get discouraged, you will compare, and criticize, and you'll get away from His Will. *Every crisis breaks out when we remove our eyes from Christ.* According to the passage in Hebrews 12, faith does not begin in men, in a pastor, or in a denomination. Jesus is the initiator of faith. Every man of God should inspire you to put your eyes on Him. Everything that begins in Him is perfected.[12] If you remain with your eyes only focused on Him, your faith will grow and be strengthened. Faith is the most powerful weapon for the extension of the Kingdom of Heaven here on earth. And the place where faith is trained, is in Him. As you have your eyes upon Him, your faith will increase and grow, and strengthen you, and it will take you to new dimensions and levels of the Kingdom.

The Church is not a place where we admire men but where we are to worship Jesus. When you're focused on Him, you freely serve and love your neighbor, because your approval and reward come from elsewhere. I am convinced that the revival the Church of the latter times will experience, has to do with a passion for Jesus like never before. Haggai has prophesied that when Jesus will be the "Desire" of the nations, then it will be the time of His return.[13] All those experiencing revivals are people, churches, and cities who have fixed their eyes on Jesus. The rest of the Christians set their eyes on those as models and try to figure out how to reach the same result in their ministries and churches. We must look to Heaven, the largest place of spiritual awakening, desire it, and wish that it will be here on earth as it is in Heaven—everyone beholding the Lamb. If you think you already know all about Jesus, let me give you some news: eternity will not have enough time for you to discover all the new aspects of His person, for He is eternal and endless. Whenever we find an open window in the Bible to see how worship is in Heaven, we discover everyone over there not being able to withdraw their gaze and admiration from He who sits on the throne. The elders, the angels, the living creatures and absolutely everything that was created, cannot help but contemplate Him and repeat over and over again: *"Holy, holy, holy."* His beauty is indescribable, and His glory is eternal. Isaiah had an encounter with God, and after that he said His name is Wonderful. This word refers to one who is worthy of being looked at, one who produces admiration and pleasure in others. For many, "being admirable" or wonderful is a quality, so we can imagine the dimension Jesus produces in those who encounter Him, if rather than a feature of His personality, "Wonderful" is His name and His identity.

I was preaching on this subject in a church and the pastor, a minister of many years, was in the front row listening. This is a notable man of God, highly respected by hundreds of other pastors, full of wisdom and anointing. When we were finishing the service, I could see that he was bowing down before the Lord. I wanted to give him the microphone for him to close the service, but he did not change his position. He stayed that way for more than half an hour. Finally, I decided to close it myself and release the people. After a while, he came towards me and hugged me, and then he said: *I saw Jesus today. I could not see Him face to face, because His glory would not let me look up, but He was in front of me. For the first time in my life, I saw Him before me. I have no words to explain what happened, I just want to worship Him.*

It is remarkable the way Christ is revealing Himself to today's "Nicodemus" who long to cross that line and become children of intimacy. Those who are willing to leave everything behind in order to be closer to His heart. There is much more available to those who hunger for Him, for those who like the people in the wilderness are raising their gaze to find His eyes of love. Jesus is the eternal revival.

His spring is inexhaustible and keeps flowing every day. In His eyes you will find the higher pleasures of His Presence which cannot be compared to any delight this world has to offer. Jesus is the superior pleasure, and as you look at Him you'll begin to be transformed more like Him. We become what we look at. So, tell me who your eyes are fixed on and I'll tell you who you will be ten years from now. This is the way for you to move from a son of religion to a son of intimacy. This was the answer Jesus gave Nicodemus. And it was at that moment that the veil was torn within this religious man. A passion erupted inside of him. He could see who was standing before him. Just as that little baby who suddenly fixed her eyes on her father, stopped crying, and began to smile. Eventually, my daughter learned to look at me, more and more often.

So, now we're ready for the next step: hearing His voice. Being a son or daughter of intimacy has to do with listening and hearing the Father. As Jesus, who did nothing but what He *saw* the Father doing, and said nothing He had not *heard* the Father saying, we can feel now His loving gaze fixed on us. It is time to listen to what His heart is shouting out loud.

On the following pages you'll not only feel His loving eyes upon you, but also you'll hear His voice freeing you. We cannot live as sons and daughters of intimacy without knowing what God says about us. So let us move in this wonderful way only walked by those who yearn to be children of intimacy, with a strong faith, initiated and perfected in Him.

PRACTICAL GUIDE CHAPTER 3

· *Eyes Fixed on the Father* ·

Questions to share in groups, cells or leadership teams:

1. What circumstances in our personal lives caused us to take our eyes off the Father?

2. What everyday situations tempt us to look away from Christ, producing discouragement and negative consequences in us? Do you recognize any idol that is cooling your love for God?

3. How can we develop a lifestyle that allows us to keep our eyes fixed on Jesus?

4. How important is a real encounter with the glory of God in the life of a believer? What are the consequences of not having it? And what are the consequences of reaching this encounter?

Personal application exercise:

Make a written prayer to God where you detail:

- Your repentance for having taken your eyes off God and having put idols in the way.

- Your desire to keep your gaze fixed on Jesus in the midst of any adverse circumstance or temporary storm.

-Your hunger and desire to know more of His glory, beauty, character, and attributes.

- Your desire to have a real and transformative encounter that produces a before and after in your life.

Persevere in this prayer and attitude until you find the answer! Ask and it will be given to you, knock and it will be opened to you, seek and you will find!

CHAPTER 4

· Eradicating the Spirit of Orphanhood ·

*All orphanhood goes away when
we hear the voice of God calling us
children, and telling us what He
feels for us.*

*Only those who are His children
can cry Abba. Only those who know
they are heard, cry out.*

*Many churches have already
become spiritual orphanages, where
people who breathe but have no
relationship with God accumulate.*

CHAPTER 4

· Eradicating the Spirit of Orphanhood
·

A friend went into an orphanage in the United States. He told me in detail about his experience over there. He met abandoned children of all ages. He described that place as one of the saddest he had ever visited. The director began guiding him through the facilities telling him of the hard work they did when they were taking in and ministering the love of God to those little rejected ones. My friend wandered around the building until he reached a place that caught his attention above any other. In this room there were many cribs, one next to another. All of a sudden, he noticed something very peculiar in there, an atrocious silence ruled the room. At a glance there were about fifty cribs, but there were no signs of life in them. The director explained to him, this was where they had the newborn babies abandoned by their parents. He asked, "Are the babies alive?" The man replied, "Sure, you can come and see them." As he approached them, he noticed that the babies were right there, most of them awake, with their eyes open, only they did not cry, they were paralyzed. He waited a few moments, but the situation remained the same. They looked sad and disoriented. However, they did not cry. Then, my friend filled with anguish, asked if what was happening was normal, "Why are the babies not crying, calling, or moaning?" The response of the man in charge of the orphanage impacted this young man's heart like mine when he told me about it. The difficult words to digest were: "Babies only cry when they know they are being heard by their parents. Once the babies feel they are not seen or heard, they stop crying. These babies have cried a lot, but they have also stopped doing it a while ago. Orphaned babies no longer call their parents." With tears in his eyes my friend related these words and at that moment the Spirit began to describe to me how the spirit of orphanhood operates in the children of religion, to sow death in their hearts and keep them away from the love of the Father.

Today, there are many who have stopped crying because they feel their Father no longer loves or listens to them. They are muted, paralyzed, and feel neither seen nor loved by God. Perhaps they have prayed for something and did not receive the desired response, and so they preferred to believe the lie that it was not taken into account by Him. The spirit of orphanhood is one of the major diabolical weapons to break the essence of a child. We find in so many places that the church does not pray, it doesn't cry, it doesn't moan, it doesn't worship. It just breathes, lives or survives.

Orphanhood is much more than the abandonment of parents; technically, it's a feeling that produces lack of value, protection, and shelter. Orphanhood is a spirit of fear that brings so much rejection that people need to find their safety and esteem in things other than the Father's arms. A spiritual orphan will seek to replace the Presence of God with ministry, money, pleasures, or even religious structures. He will try to find value in what he does, which is temporary, instead of who he is, which is eternal. In so many nations of the world we find this spirit destroying the purposes of hundreds of men and women. *Many churches have already become spiritual orphanages, where people who breathe but have no relationship with God accumulate.* Paul describes this spirit as follows:

> *"For you did not receive the spirit of bondage again to fear, but you received the Spirit of adoption by whom we cry out, «Abba, Father.» The Spirit Himself bears witness with our spirit that we are children of God."*
> **Romans 8:15-16, NKJV**

The Father has a plan. It's visiting that orphanage in your soul and adopting you. He will break any barrier and, finally, He will bring His warmth to your spirit. He will answer a thousand times to your question: Do you still love me? *I love you so much that I have given my only begotten Son for you.*[14] As you read the following pages, you will receive the spirit of adoption taking your life and you will cry again. Only those who know they are heard by their father cry out. Only those who are children pray. If you pay attention, you can begin to hear the voice of the Spirit testifying to your spirit: *You are a son, a daughter, you are a child of God, you are not the child of a religion, and you are loved from eternity and chosen as the son or daughter of the living God.* There is an emptiness within you that cannot be filled by natural, ministerial or business success. Being a great minister, or being recognized by crowds can't quench your hunger for inner love. You will never find value, protection and shelter in things other than the arms of Him who designed every fiber of your being and who drew plans of fullness for you to walk in. The only thing that brings peace to your soul is to see the Heavens open and to hear the voice of your Father saying, *You are my beloved child.*

"You Are My Child and I like You"

"And the Holy Spirit came upon Him in a physical manifestation that resembled a dove. A voice echoed out from heaven: «You are My Son, the Son I love, and in You I take great pleasure.»"

Luke 3:22, The Voice version

Jesus begins His earthly ministry with two clear statements from the Father. The first one is who He is. The Father needs to establish the identity of Jesus in who He is, and not in what He will do. Many will call Him a teacher, some a prophet, some a good pastor, an apostle, or an evangelist. In fact, they are all titles given to Jesus in the Bible. But the foundation of all His ministry must be based on what the Father thinks of Him, and not on hierarchical positions or ministerial functions. It will not be miracles and signs that will define Jesus. It will not be what people feel for Him, at times they will applaud Him and suddenly they will crucify Him. The Father might have said, *This is my chosen Savior, my Supernatural Superhero,* or something like that. However, He decides to give Him, in plain sight, the greatest title a person can receive: *"Beloved Son."* Many times I have asked myself, why did not the Father use this ministerial presentation before the people to declare Jesus the Messiah? God has shown me that Jesus, who was tempted in all things after our likeness,[15] could not have attained His Messianic purpose if His identity was not based on what the Father thought of Him. In other words, we cannot achieve our purpose if we don't build on the foundation that we are His beloved sons and daughters.

The second statement the Father wants to make clear is *what produces a son in His heart*. The words used are "well-pleased", "great pleasure", they come from "experiencing pleasure." The Father is saying, *You produce pleasure in me. When I see you my heart rejoices, beyond what you will produce in others, you must know what happens in my heart when I think of you.* All orphanhood goes away when we hear the voice of God calling us children, and telling us what He feels for us. He calls you by name. A dear friend puts it this way: "Empires are counted by numbers, but in the Kingdom of God everyone is known by name." Since my childhood I have heard that God loves us. However, I could only understand the dimension of this truth when I clearly heard the Father telling me so. It was a few years ago, and this experience transformed my life. The preacher was giving a message about God's love. All of a sudden I stopped listening to the human voice, and an inner and supernatural sound thrilled me: *Mariano, you are my beloved son, and I like you.* God likes me! I used to believe He was obligated to love me, because He had no choice. But then, I entered into the reality of the pleasure that the Father feels for His children. It was so liberating for my soul to know that God enjoys me, even in my process of growing and maturing. That day, I stopped trying to please everyone. The Creator likes me, He calls me His son, and that's enough for me. This truth eradicated all orphanhood from me. Today I live free, trying to bless and love all who come across my way, because I know that when I go to bed each night my Father will be watching me and feeling pleasure. This has nothing to do with what we do, but with who *we are*.

Far from being a permission to sin, or to do whatever we want, this truth generates a greater responsibility in those who know that the eyes of the Father are fixed on us and that they are full of expectancy as they look at every step we take.

I remember, when Conie was born, I stared into her eyes and said, *You are my daughter, I love you and it gives me pleasure to look at you. No matter what you will do in your life, you may be a great minister or prophet, or who knows what you will be. But beyond that, you will always be my daughter, it doesn't matter what people think of you, I will always be there when you need me, in good and bad times, I believe in you and I love you.* Last week, I was about to go on a ministerial trip and I had to catch a flight at dawn. I went over to her room, looked at her asleep, and I began to cry with pleasure. It had nothing to do with her successes or mistakes (in fact that day she had not behaved well and I had to chide her). However, seeing the face of my beloved daughter resting lit my heart with a unique and extreme love. As I watched her sleeping, I heard my Father's whisper of love in my spirit saying, *Many nights I do this very same thing with you, I look at you while you sleep, and you overwhelm me with pleasure. Although sometimes I have to scold you for your mistakes, I feel an extreme love every time I look at you. Neither angels nor archangels nor any living thing can produce this in my heart, only my children.*

It is imperative for a child of the wind to have his identity anchored in the heart of God. We cannot reach the dimension Jesus spoke about to Nicodemus unless we know how He defines us. If you don't listen to what the Father says about you, you will worry about what someone else says. If you don't find your value in what He thinks and feels for you, you will look for it elsewhere. You need to affirm these words in the depths of your being. You are His son or daughter and He likes you. He has thoughts of peace and not of evil for your life.[16] You will be tempted again and again to get out of the comfort of divine love, but you must eradicate those spirits and secure your heart in the eternal truth that you are enjoyed by Him.

The Temptation of Orphanhood

After this wonderful event, the devil comes in person in order to tempt Jesus. If you are dangerous to the kingdom of darkness, Satan will send a legion of demons to slow you down. But, if you have heard the Father's voice and accepted your identity as His son or daughter, he will appear in person and he will try to abort your purpose, for it is a serious case for him. The Gospel of Luke, in chapter 4, from verses 3 to 9, show us how Satan tempts Jesus. He tries to bring in the spirit of orphanhood a couple of times: *"If You are the Son of God..."* In other words he is saying, *So your heavenly Father calls you His beloved son? Prove it! Work miracles, I want to see how powerful you are.* Satan tempts Jesus to place His value in His power. He wants to take Him from *being* (Son of God) to *doing* (turning the stone into bread). This is the temptation for those who feel empty of God's fatherhood in their hearts, they will try to demonstrate their value through manifestation of power, miracles, good ministrations or recognition. This is how the spirit of religiosity works. The children of religion, for they are not satisfied within their soul, will try to feel secure through the approval of denomination, hierarchies, accumulation of knowledge or reputation. This was the great problem of the Pharisees. They believed they first were ministers, priests or guardians of the Law before being children of God. Then they crucified the highest expression of God's love incarnated in Jesus.

The Lord responds to Satan by affirming His value in what the Father has said, and in what is written about Him, and not in his questions. More than once the devil will put question marks to what God has told us in our intimacy. Again and again he will come and say to us: *So are you God's son? So the Father feels pleasure when He sees you? So why does this or that happen to you? Why are you not used by Him with power?* Your response must be based on what your Father has declared to you and in what is written about you, and not by temporal circumstances. They do not dictate your identity, but what the Creator of the immovable has said, it does. Then the spirit of orphanhood will find no place in your heart and it will be stripped away. Now you have freedom to worship and claim all of God's promises. The Holy Spirit is shouting this truth to you today.[17] You need to affirm your identity in what He who designed you says about you. Begin to live to please the Father, like Jesus did. May your goal every morning, evening, and night be to honor the expectations He has for you. That's what Jesus did:

> *"And He who sent Me is with Me. The Father has not left*
> *Me alone, for I always do those things that please Him."*
> **John 8:29, NKJV**

This is the key to a true life of intimacy with the Father, and the foundation for a ministry full of purpose, power, and signs. God can entrust His treasures to those who first know that they are His children, and who overcome the temptation of orphanhood. However, the religious system is based on you loving the glory of men and their favor more than God's. Look at these rulers who were more interested in being part of the Pharisee regime than the Heavenly denomination:

> *"Nevertheless even among the rulers many believed in*
> *Him, but because of the Pharisees they did not confess*
> *Him, lest they should be put out of the synagogue; for*
> *they loved the praise of men more than the praise*
> *of God."*
> **John 12:42-43, NKJV**

The Spirit of adoption will make you love the glory of God more than the glory of men. It will only satisfy you to hear the voice of the Father. In the place where you are now reading this book, listen to the testimony within you. Your Father likes you, nothing can separate you from His love. Live no longer for anything else other than to please Him. This revolution of love within you will fill your mouth with a new song and a fresh cry. Even in the most difficult and most solitary moments, you can always say "Abba", and you will see Heaven descending in the midst of your need. But remember, only those who know they are heard by the Father are the ones who cry out. Let me describe the first moment in human history when this word was recorded as a prayer to God.

Abba

This is not the kind of prayer that you learn in the synagogues of Israel. The teachers of the Law could not justify those words theologically. No one had ever referred to God that way in the past. The cup containing the wrath of God for the sin of man is served. No human could drink it and be immune from its consequences. I mean, just one. There is Jesus. He is alone in Gethsemane. His close friends fell asleep. He makes it clear that He will not drink the cup because of His own choice, but because He was born to meet the expectations of His Father. He is under so much pressure that a few minutes ago He stopped sweating water, His pores are shedding blood now. At this moment, He doesn't feel like singing any hymn, and every prayer He tries to say seems to be locked. There is something in His heart that He just can't get out. His mind was filled with loneliness and anguish. The temptation of orphanhood seems to knock on His door. However, His agitated sighs become a sound composed of four letters. When He utters them like a whisper, a heat floods down His being releasing a peace within Him that strengthens Him for what is coming. What is that word? *ABBA.*

> *"...but you received the Spirit of adoption by whom we*
> *cry out, «Abba, Father.»"*
>
> **Romans 8:15**

This is the first expression a Jewish child exclaims as he begins to speak. His first word is Abba. It means: *my Daddy*, Daddy. In Argentina we have an expression that children use whenever they ask for the arms of their father, it is *upa.* The little one extends his arms looking for security and identity. He belongs there. That is Abba. There is no expression of love and dependence, more genuine than this.

Religiosity has described a distant God to us. We do not find any difficulty to see Him as Creator, as Master, and as Lord. God has manifested Himself as a Deliverer in rescuing the Israelites from Egyptian slavery.

I visited Israel on ministerial trips and it has always struck me to see the Jews clamoring on the Wailing Wall or other holy places. With passion they worship the great and fearsome God, the Owner of the universe and the galaxies, but they crucify the idea of a God who manifests Himself as their close Father. They love the stories of God opening the sea in Egypt, or making manna fall from Heaven into the desert, the fire on Carmel, or the plagues. But, they nailed to Calvary a God who manifests Himself as their Friend, Husband, and Father. It's evident they have no problems with His greatness, but they do with His closeness. And even today many Christians have the same difficulty. They are thrilled to sing hymns about His greatness, which is beautiful, but they remain silent and watch as we worship with declarations of intimate love or romance. Some believe that it's disrespectful towards God to treat Him that way, but I believe there is no greater disrespect than not understanding the heart of God when sending His own Son to establish the idea of a close and loving God. By giving Jesus, His beloved Son, the Living God gave the Earth a revolutionary revelation, He is a close Father. However, many of them rejected Him. The idea they had of a distant God, did not allow them to recognize Him when He was in front of them. Do we have the same problem today? We have God before our eyes and we do not recognize Him because we don't have the right revelation. The Jews saw Him as a God of battles, victories, judgments, and power. However, God believed they were too far away, and decided to reveal Himself as Father. Jesus is the Father's hook, who draws the heart of man towards Him. Abba is one of the most beautiful expressions of closeness and love that a son can express. It breaks the distance that religion proposes. *Only those who are His children can cry Abba. Only those who know they are heard, cry out.* When we had the spirit of fear, we did not pray, we could not approach the Father freely. He embraced us and called us His children. His Spirit continually preaches now to our spirit that we are His little children, our voice is heard, we can cry, we can call.

The Bible is full of stories of children of religion who were transformed into sons and daughters of intimacy. In this book we will analyze several of them. Jesus sets you free so you can set others free. When you receive such a dimension of God's love for your life, you just can't live for anything other than for others to experience it. I'm not writing here from theories but from experiences that I have verified through the years. I have seen God transforming religious ones into close friends in many places. I have seen orphans being converted into sons and daughters of intimacy through the Spirit of adoption many times. Today they have become fathers and mothers for this generation. I can feel this process is being experienced by every person who has this message from Heaven in their hands.

In the next chapter we will go deeper into the Spirit of adoption. You can meet His loving gaze now, and hear His sweet voice releasing your inner self. Now is the time for this new identity to be sealed with fire within you.

PRACTICAL GUIDE CHAPTER 4

· *Eradicating the Spirit of Orphanhood* ·

Questions to share in groups, cells or leadership teams:

1. How can we discover what the Father says and feels about us?

2. In what ways does Satan tempt us to question our identity as children and thus introduce spiritual orphanhood?

3. What relationship is there between the lack of cry or spiritual paralysis of the Church and orphanhood?

4. How can we guide others to experience the Father's love that activates them?

5. Why is it so difficult to see God as our Abba?

Personal application exercise:

Take some time to pray and ask God to reveal to you what He thinks and feels about you. After doing so, listen to His words within yourself and in a spirit of faith, write them down below. I advise you not to fall into the temptation to believe that it is your imagination, but to be guided by His Spirit. Remember that a person is not truly free until he hears the Father tell him who he is and how much He loves him.

My son/daughter, ____

CHAPTER 5

· Experiencing the Divine Fatherhood ·

Spiritual children need idols, but mature sons and daughters prefer someone close to them who walks with them.

True freedom is not doing whatever we want, but rather the Father doing whatever He wants in us.

The path of intimacy with God is a way of death and resurrection. Every time you die to something that God asks you for, something glorious rises up.

CHAPTER 5

· *Experiencing the Divine Fatherhood* ·

Every year, with our MiSion Ministry, we develop a worship conference called *Intimacy with the Beloved.* In the last decade, hundreds and thousands of people have come from different cities and nations. Since its first edition, we've had deep times of intimate communion with God, insightful adoration, and revelation of the beauty of His person. Each one is a different and glorious encounter. Last year, I received a striking testimony. A woman from our church named Fabiana had made her plans to attend this divine appointment. A couple of months earlier she learned that she was pregnant with her second child. She and her husband were very happy. The same day the conference was scheduled to start, she went to get a medical checkup. The doctor passed the ultrasound down her abdomen and she quickly realized by his face that something was not right. He repeated the action several times. Uncertainty transformed those minutes into an eternity. Finally and helplessly, she asked the question: "Doctor, is there any problem?" The doctor's face confirmed the worst. The baby was dead. There was no pulse, no heart activity, no movement, and no sign of life. With an indescribable anguish, Fabiana saw her world collapsing within seconds. The medical report indicated that gestation had been stopped several days prior. The doctor instructed her to rest that weekend, and that the baby would probably be expelled spontaneously, and, if this did not happen, she should return the following Tuesday for a procedure to remove it. Fabiana left the doctor's office devastated. Later that day she testified before the whole church that she felt she was dying. However, she decided to go and weep in the Presence of God, and she attended the night of *Intimacy with the Beloved*. Can you imagine what I'm describing here? She was going to the Presence of God with a dead baby in her womb. She told me that she threw herself at Jesus' feet that night and cried deeply in a corner of the auditorium. She declared things like, "Jesus, where can I go other than to Your Presence? I know the power that raised You from the dead operates in me. I know You can bring my baby back to life, as you did with Lazarus. It's never late for You. But, even if that doesn't happen, You will always be my Beloved. Here I am in Your intimacy."

The weekend went by. On Tuesday she returned to the doctor because nothing he said had happened. When the experienced doctor began to perform the tests and check the position to produce the extraction, there was something unusual in Fabiana's womb. After passing the instruments over her womb, and making himself sure, he excitedly exclaimed: *Your baby is alive. I do not understand what happened. Her heart rate is normal. I have never, in all my life as a doctor, seen something like that.* As he compared the studies and images with the ones from four days ago, every detail was more supernatural. The baby was not only moving and her heart beating but, in proportion, she had grown up in four days as much as a baby grows in weeks. Fabiana gave me the studies and the ultrasounds as a valid sign of the power of Jesus today to raise the dead. I have them still, and I show them to anyone who asks me for them, simply to see clearly the power of God. It overwhelms me to observe those images. You can see the entire description of a dead baby in the first report with many details, and then the description of life on the next ultrasound four days later. As I write this book, Genesis has just been born healthy, vital, and whole. Her existence is a living testimony of the life that flows in the Presence of God. When a person decides to approach intimacy with the Father, she is taken by a spirit of life. Genesis is literally a daughter of intimacy, vitalized in the Father's lap. The spirit of religion produces death, while the bosom of the Father emanates life. Orphanhood produces sterility, but within the intimate ones there is fertility. A symptom of a child of intimacy is their fruit. Through them, the Father's support is seen. Many seem to know too much about doctrine and theology, but they have no fruit, neither spiritual children nor disciples. So it happened with the Pharisees. When Nicodemus crossed through that barrier, he experienced the Spirit of adoption. That day a part of him died, but something much greater resurrected. This Spirit brought life where there was death, and empowered him to see the Kingdom of God and become a main character of the divine purpose.

Accepting the Spirit of Adoption

"And because you are sons, God has sent forth the Spirit
of His Son into your hearts, crying out, «Abba, Father!»
Therefore you are no longer a slave but a son, and if a
son, then an heir of God through Christ."
Galatians 4:6-7, NKJV

When we accept our identity as sons and daughters through the Spirit of adoption provided by Jesus, we are legal partakers of the inheritance reserved for those born from God. "Heirs" may take legal possession of all that their Father possesses as they own that by right. In this heritage are included the elements of the Heavenly Kingdom: blessings, life, power, and healing. Although everyone knows the meaning of the word "heir," one of its definitions draw my attention: *One who presents the characteristics of their parents or ancestors.* It is not only an inheritance in material and spiritual goods but also in the features of His attributes. Those who receive the mantle of God's paternity, by eradicating orphanhood, can partake of the divine nature.

> *"Seeing that His divine power has granted to us*
> *everything pertaining to life and godliness, through the*
> *true knowledge of Him who called us by His own glory*
> *and excellence. For by these He has granted to us His*
> *precious and magnificent promises, so that by them*
> *you may become partakers of the divine nature, having*
> *escaped the corruption that is in the world by lust."*
> **2 Peter 1:3-4, NASB**

By escaping the corruption of an orphan identity, we can legally access the power of Heaven and the nature of the Father. However, the question is: Why are there only a few people who make use of this legal inheritance? Why are there so few "Christians" who reflect the nature of the Father?

The key to becoming children of intimacy and heirs of the eternal legacy is to accept the Spirit of adoption. God entered the orphanage where we were alone and spiritually dead. He broke into that place of rejection, silence, and abandonment where we could not say Abba.

Without deserving it, He called us His children by the pure affection of His will. He gave us a new name, last-name, and inheritance. He transformed our future of pain and death into a destiny of glory. He invited us permanently into His delighting room, where we can live as it is in Heaven, but on earth. He gave us a new home and crowned us with favor and mercy. He gave us back the voice and the song. Now, why are there many who cannot live in this dimension of love?

I know of an adoption case that I want to describe here. A marriage full of love adopted a girl. They explained to me how adoption and orphaning work in practice. When she was a little girl they chose her, they gave her protection, and a last name. With all this, they gave her their love and provision, and she was called: *daughter.* Throughout her childhood they gave the little girl a passionate love, they provided for all her needs. She was raised, educated, bought gifts, and accompanied in the most important moments. In short, they loved her in every way a parent can love a daughter.

However, in a moment of her adolescence, the girl entered a serious crisis of identity. When she learned she was adopted, she fought hard against the orphanhood her biological parents had bequeathed her. She could not enjoy the love she was receiving because of the pain of the past. She lived several years not feeling worthy of the love of her adoptive parents. She decided to change her last name, and although she lived under the same roof, she renegaded the inheritance of her parents. Her phrases were, *I am not like you, and I am not your daughter. Even if you try everything, I will never be your daughter. My reality is different, my biological parents abandoned me and there is nothing you can do to change this.* Her parents struggled to make her understand that she was their daughter and not an orphan. But, it seemed that all attempts were in vain. Imagine how the Father's heart feels when we struggle to accept His fatherhood and we resist to receive His love and inheritance. Being a daughter and heir, she lived for years as an orphan. This state led her to depression. She was legally a daughter, but she decided to live as an orphan. Similarly, there are hundreds of Christians who live in the Father's house but do not accept His love. They remain tied to their past and cannot let themselves be embraced by the Spirit of adoption. A professional expert in these cases, explained to me that adoption begins when parents choose a person as a child, but is completed when the child chooses and accepts them as parents. If the latter does not happen, the circle doesn't close and this person will always feel like an orphan. I know that many times it's not easy to fight against the abandonment and rejection that people have caused us, but Jesus has opened a way of love and restoration that we need to embrace. He came to manifest that the Father is close and active in every matter of your life. He is willing to surround you with His arms of love until He conquers your pain and you call Him Abba. He already calls you son or daughter, but the circle closes when you can call Him Father. He will try a thousand ways to attract you, but you must yield to His love and accept His inheritance. There are countless treasures that you will receive by understanding this eternal truth. The Jews preferred to see God as the hero who freed them, and crucified the Father who came to love them intimately. This happens to many Christians today. They have no problem accepting the sacrifice of Jesus for their salvation, but they struggle with receiving His constant Father's love that activates an inheritance of delight and glory in this life. When I was a kid, I wanted my dad to be a superhero, but when I was growing up, I realized that what I needed was a close father to hold me and affirm me in every moment of my life. *Spiritual children need idols, but mature sons and daughters prefer someone close to them who walks with them.* God is Almighty, but He is also "all close" and "all loving." Recognizing and accepting this living truth will introduce you to a new relationship with the Father. Your inheritance will be activated and you will be able to call Him Abba.

Our Father

In the Jewish context, the word "father" takes on a value far more transcendent than in Western culture. Many Jews are surnamed as *son of: the name of their father.* For example, I met a Jew named Eli Bar David. "Bar" means "son of." Then the translation would be Eli Son of David. His father's name is David. Paternity in Jewish culture brings identity. One can know where he comes from, what rights he has, and his life will be determined by who his father is. In this context, understanding our identity as sons and daughters of God is extremely important. If you are a child of religion or tradition, your identity, your heritage, and your purpose are distorted. Jesus said that when praying we are to say "Our Father" to God. This should bring a new revelation of our identity, purpose, destiny, and heritage to us. Imagine what such a statement caused in the Jewish context. He was introducing the Spirit of adoption. In other words, from that moment they were children of God, and they had to begin their prayers declaring the divine paternity.

One of the most outstanding purposes of Jesus' ministry was to bring the revelation of heavenly paternity to the Jews and Gentiles. The word "father" appears two hundred and thirty-five times in the gospels just coming from the mouth of Jesus. He constantly made public His intimacy with the Father. He made it clear that His Father's wishes prevailed in all His decisions and actions. Each day was an opportunity to execute the will of the Father on earth. When people filled His agenda with daily commitments, He would escape to the wilderness or some mountain to pray to His Father. If it was necessary, He would spend all night in His Abba's lap. He established this place of love to be His beginning and end, His foundation and destiny, where He came from and where He was going.

"Father"

I heard the teaching of a pastor, who inspires me, saying that we all need a "father," a "dad" and a "daddy." It was a concept that brought a lot of wisdom to my life. The "father" is a figure of authority that is so necessary for all of us to have. God is our Father and this requires our obedience without objections. Spiritual authority is a weak area in today's Church. We prefer independence and self-sufficiency. Having a "Father" implies that we cannot do what we want, we need to ask for permission and be sure that every decision we make is endorsed by Him. This is a way of blessing and grace. *True freedom is not doing whatever we want, but rather the Father doing whatever He wants in us.* Jesus related to God as His "Father." The love He showed through ubmitting Himself to the Father and obeying His authority was a constant in His life. Neither the anointing nor the power made Him independent. He was always dependent and acknowledged that He was not on His own, but obeyed the authority of the One who had sent Him. I know about some cultures where this paternal aspect of the "father" as a figure of authority and respect is highly marked. In many Latin American countries the children relate to their father as "sir." It is great to have the concept of father so clear and to give them the respect they deserve. The same happens with God. It is essential that we never lose the fear and reverence the Master of eternity deserves. However, we also need to go deeper into our relationship with Him and understand that He is also our "Dad."

"Dad"

"Dad" is a fatherhood figure that implies more confidence and intimacy than the concept of "father." When we understand that God is our authority and deserves our respect and fear, then we can relate to Him as our "Dad." It is so important that a "dad" never cease to be a "father," or vice versa. One feeds the other. It's "dad" who gives us validation, acceptance, and affirmation. Our character is determined by the influence of our "dad." He gets close enough to give us the stability we need to lose our fears. He gives us a pat on our back when we act correctly. He is the number one fan in our areas of competence and he boasts of the child He has before others. He makes us feel confident saying that what we do matters. People who have enjoyed the affirmation of their earthly dad, they commonly feel safe and strong. They often think, "If my dad thinks well of me, I have enough." Many times I have to counsel children of pastors or ministers. I ask if they have felt enough assessment and validation from their parents or they would have liked to have more. The answer surprises me. In almost 100% of the cases, they would have needed more affirmation than demands. Many pastors, in their quest for their children not to go astray, believe that with demand and control, they will succeed. The result is resounding, most of the pastor's children end up apart. They need a "father" who is also a "dad."

If you have not had a dad to affirm you, stay calm, your heavenly Dad is your number one fan. He boasts with the angels about you. He has disarmed the heavenly order to come to earth in your ransom. He got a "tattoo" with your name on the palm of His hand (before you sting me, His Word says that He has your name sculpted there). When someone wants to condemn you and accuse you, He remarks that no one can mess with His chosen ones. He rejoices in your joys and He grieves with your troubles. You cannot flee from His love, because He surrounds you behind and before, and He chases you everywhere. Whenever you drift too far, He pulls out His ropes of love to draw you close (perhaps these words are acting as irresistible bonds even now).

If we conjugate these two facets of God, a "Father" and a "Dad," it is wonderful what we can experience. Those who have only related to the first aspect of God, live condemned and demanded, they never reach the parameter their "Father" demands of them. They are always at fault and feel guilty. They adopt the lifestyle of feeling like victims, they enjoy the mercy of God but they lose His favor. Do you feel that way? You urgently need to see God as your "Dad" who enjoys you.

On the other hand, those who have only experienced the aspect of God as "Dad" usually believe that everything they do is good, they never experience correction, and therefore they go from freedom to debauchery. They do not understand that the "Father" grieves for disobedience and His heart suffers with bad attitudes. Their hearts are filled with pride and they justify their bad attitudes by arguing for an unreal support of God (they often use phrases such as "God told me such a thing..." or "I felt God this or that..."). It is not that God does not speak to us or give us the feeling of His heart, but if this is not backed up by the character and obedience shaped by the revelation of "God the Father" that produces a dangerous imbalance.

When we get the revelation that He is our "Father" and our "Dad" it flows into our character everything that is necessary to relate healthily to God and to our neighbor. We can enjoy His corrections and His affirmation. However, there is a more intimate level in our paternal relationship with God and I consider it to be the most important one, "Daddy."

"Daddy"

As we saw in the previous chapter, "Abba" means "Daddy." Only when we access this level of intimacy with the Father and we call Him Abba, we receive the love that nourishes and strengthens our life. It's here, where the facet of "Father" and "Dad" are fed. "Daddy" is the one who hugs us and whispers in our ear that he loves us. He's the one who kisses us and smiles when he sees us. It's incredible to see how, in many cultures, men can be "fathers" and "dads" without being "daddies." They fear losing their manhood if they play with their children, kiss them or let them fall asleep in their lap. Like them, children think that calling "daddy" to their father is a sign of weakness. True weakness is produced by children who cannot call God "Abba." In this way, they can't access a deeper and more vital degree in their intimacy with God. Feeling the warmth of Daddy's chest cannot be compared to any other sensation in the world. When Jesus teaches the parable of the prodigal son, leaving the highest expression of the nature of the Father's love well-seated, He said that when the son repented, his "daddy" embraced him and kissed him. Kissing is the deeper act of worship. Only those who experience this level of intimacy with God can establish a contact with Him. "Contact" means "with touch." God wants you to feel His touch of love, and He wants you to be able to say in His ear, "I love you Abba."

Now you can understand why, in Gethsemane, Jesus does not say "Father" to God in His prayer (He Himself had taught the disciples to pray that way), He doesn't say "Father," but He exclaims "Daddy" instead. Only those who are children adopted by divine Love can call Him Abba. The Spirit is the One who brings conviction within you that you can relate to God in this way. It is time for you to experience God's Fatherhood in fullness. Only those who know they are heard cry out, and you are one of them. Your words are heard in the Heavens. Feed your spirit with the necessary faith and begin calling. Cry if necessary, but let your voice be heard. The Father wants to play with you, He wants to affirm you and also whispers in your ear how much He loves you. "Abba" is not a magic word, but if you begin to express it with revelation and wisdom, you will enter into the depths of God's love. I encourage you to use this key of intimacy, the door will open before you, and you will find yourself there, in the place where only few want to enter. Abba!

Spirit of Life

The path of intimacy with God is a way of death and resurrection. Every time you die to something that God asks you for, something glorious rises up. When you reject orphanhood and accept the intimate fatherhood of God, all that was dead begins to live. The divine dreams and purposes are awakened, and the healing, restoration, and delights of His Presence begin to flourish. If you've struggled for years with the feeling of being loved and adopted by God, I think it's a good time for you to give up. God has never lost a battle. Finally, His love will overcome and possess you. The life of the Spirit will begin to revitalize your interior. You will become a giver of life to everything you touch. By calling God "Abba," the divine inheritance will be activated in your life and the nature of the Father will begin to run through your entire being. Your words will begin to be spirit and life, producing supernatural results for natural problems.

I invite you to continue to advance in this wonderful way. As you stare into Abba's eyes of love, you will discover a gaze that will consume all that is wrong in you. His gaze and His love will make all the religiosity die in your life. I can feel it in my spirit: A new son or daughter of intimacy is about to be born.

PRACTICAL GUIDE CHAPTER 5

· *Experiencing the Divine Fatherhood* ·

Questions to share in groups, cells or leadership teams:

1. Do you recognize people who were adopted by God, but struggle to adopt God as their Father? What characteristics do they have?

2. In your relationship with God, which of the three facets of God's fatherhood do you have the most difficulty relating to (Father, Dad or Daddy)?

3. What things is God asking you to die to in order to experience the fullness of His fatherhood?

4. How can we guide others to know the full revelation of the fatherhood of God?

Personal application exercise:

Write a sentence that expresses your understanding of each facet of God as Father, Dad, and Abba, and declare it audibly. Focus on the revelation of each aspect and write specifically about each dimension of God's fatherhood. Go deeper into the area where you find it most difficult to relate to Him.

Loving father _______________________________

____

____

____

____

Dear Dad _______________________________

____

____

____

____

____

Abba _______________________________

____

____

____

Loving father _______________________________

____

CHAPTER 6

· Seen and Loved by the Father ·

*Jacob did not fit the clothes
of Esau, David did not fit the
armor of Saul, and you will
never be comfortable dressed
like someone you were not
created to be.*

*It takes Satan a lifetime to
corrupt someone's identity, but
it takes God only one night to
restore it.*

*The ties of orphanhood rot away
when we understand the truth
that the Father does not take
off His eyes from us despite our
mistakes and flights.*

CHAPTER 6

· *Seen and Loved by the Father* ·

I saw a great potential in him. He had talents, gifts, and a passion for God. People liked being close to him. He was a youth leader in his church and many followed and sought him out. He was also a worship leader. A beautiful voice combined with a great anointing. God had clearly equipped him to be someone special in the advancement of the Kingdom on earth.

However, he did not see himself that way. Each time we met to chat, he showed himself to be someone who was unsuccessful, frustrated, and with a totally distorted self-image. As if looking at himself in a broken mirror, something or someone was telling him he was someone else, different to the one we all saw. They were two different beings in the same body. One of them, who I saw ministering and serving God; the other one, who chatted with me alone every week. He used to cry, complain, and ask for explanations of why God used other people and not him. I affirmed, advised, and ministered him on the very evident truth of who he was and how God saw him. In a few days, however, he returned to the same state again. I had the feeling that there was something broken inside him and I did not know how to repair it. What was it that made this warrior feel like a victim? Why could he not receive the identity that God was bestowing upon him? One which we all saw, but instead, he exchanged it for such an unreal and false image of who he was.

Finally, one day he came shattered into my office. After a little chat he exploded, and confessed to me that he had been abused by his father in childhood. His struggle against rejection had been born in that event. He had been defined by that action. No matter what God or all humanity told him, he was already affected. From that day on, he would live his whole life with his new name: "abused." There are events that happen in our lives that define us. Whether we are responsible or not for what happened, there are events that baptize our identity in such a way that it seems to be irreversible. The teenage girl who was fondled by a schoolmate, will believe her whole life that she is more a beautiful and attractive body than a priceless treasure. The teenager who discovered pornography at an early age, will be affected in his identity as someone correct in the public, but a monster in the secret. The boy who was raped or abused, will accept that fact defining him as homosexual. He who grew up seeing family violence, will be violent. He who had immoral parents, will justify his lasciviousness with what he inherited. That girl who lost her parents as a child, will be a fighter and a warrior. The facts and circumstances are a strong and indelible voice that determine the identity of the people. Many times it's something that happened to us that marks who we are. That afternoon I told this lad that he was not what that terrible circumstance had condemned him to be, but what the Father said about him. At some point in our life we need to be redefined by what God says about us. Jesus was defined by the Father: "This is my beloved Son and in Him I feel pleasure." I guided this beloved child of God to a transcendent decision: "Today you have to decide what voice you are going to hear, what God says about you or what the things that 'happened to you' are declaring over you. Which one do you believe? Which one of the two are really you?" After this, there were three hours—by clock—in which this man cried in a corner of the office. That day, the little boy who had been abused died, and a son established by the Voice of God was born. He could return to his original essence, as God had designed him before he was corrupted. Today this person is a tremendous pastor who is used by God to liberate and restore many. He was redefined and redirected by God. From that day on, he no longer listened to the voices that wanted to confuse him, but he allowed the essence of the Eternal to fill his life and determine his identity.

Jacob, a Deceiver or Father of a Nation?

There are many people who were affected by an experience with their father. A bad relationship with your earthly father can damage your whole life. The same thing happens in the spiritual world. Not having the right revelation of God as a Father can produce a spiritual trap that is impossible to get through, and that will negatively determine your identity. A symptom of the children of religion is that they do not feel loved or seen by the Father. For this reason, they need recognition and appreciation in religious structures and in men, although none of this can satisfy the need to be contemplated and enjoyed by God.

In the Bible we have many cases that argue this point. I'd like to talk to you about Jacob. His story is exciting. Everyone knows him by the meaning of his name: the deceiver. That's what everyone called him.

However, throughout his life we see how God visited him over and over again to tell him who he really was and the glorious purpose He had with his life and his generations. Although the world defined him by the name his parents had given him because of a human circumstance, he was loved and seen by God and He had chosen him as the "father of a nation." In spite of this, Jacob always fought between the identity the circumstances proposed him, and what God said about him. He had a hard time understanding his divine identity. God did not stop until He defined Jacob according to His plan. He visited him in arid places, tents, distant lands, mountains, night and day, until He succeeded in overcoming him with His love. I would like to tell you that no matter what your parents, other people, friends or humanity say about you, what matters is what the Father thinks. He will visit you over and over, in every place and circumstance until the voice of the world is finally consumed, and until you experience what your Creator says of you. He chose you and He has a plan to carry out through your life. Even if the earth calls you a deceiver, He will seek you in deserts, and foreign lands; He will come to encounter you even though you are fleeing because of your mistakes, and He will visit you at night to transform your way of walking, your identity, and He will give direction to your destiny.

Stealing His Brother's Blessing

Let's look at Jacob's life from the beginning. He always lived according to his identity. Time after time he tried to get blessings and be "somebody" because he did not really know what God thought of him. He tried to fill the emptiness of his soul in many ways. He repeatedly pretended in order to achieve the acceptance of others because he suffered from internal rejection. First, he stole the blessing from his brother. He was so dissatisfied with who he was that he longed for what "others" (in this case his brother) had. The children of religion are defined by the world and do not feel whole. That is why they live by envying what others have. They want the ministry, the anointing, and sometimes even the wife of others. They are capable of doing whatever they can to get the blessing. They steal what God gave to others through criticism, obscure strategies, and malicious attitudes. When someone is being raised up by God, they are looking for ways to slow down his process because they feel inferior. Even when they get the approval from the others, they feel unsatisfied, just as Jacob did. Have you stolen someone's blessing? It only takes an attitude of envy or criticism to achieve it. Proverbs 14:30 says that *"...envy is rottenness to the bones."* No matter what you achieve out of envy, there will be no blessing in that. Jacob obtained the birthright by deceiving his brother for a plate of lentils. Has this joy changed anything in his life? Absolutely nothing. He continued to deceive and flee away his whole life. As we will see at the end of this story, his soul was not satiated. Have you seen people who get things and not feel satisfied? This happens because their identity is corrupted. They need to be redefined by God. Ministerial and religious achievements cannot satisfy their inner desire, the only thing that can satisfy them is meeting His loving eyes and listening to what God thinks of them.

Dressing Like Another to Get the Blessing

Jacob managed to obtain the birthright of Esau, yet he went for more. His next step was to disguise himself like his brother to obtain his father's blessing. Have you seen people who disguise themselves to gain the favor of men? They believe that if they dress as religion says, or if they sing or play like the fashion minister, or if they speak like another preacher and live in the calling of someone else, they will get the blessing. These children of religion pursue approval at any price. They are capable of losing their unique creativity and essence, and disguise themselves as "whatever the system blesses." This is what Jacob did. What was the result? He got the favor of his father, yet he lived fleeing through deserts and foreign lands. Instead of living the life of a blessed man, he became a fugitive. There is a lost creativity in the Church today. Everyone wants to be like someone else. Jesus was unique and creative. When Nicodemus approached Him, he said, *"No one can do these signs that You do."* When our identity is affirmed in the Father, we are not afraid of the new, nor of doing what no one else does. A creative anointing is unleashed. I believe in a generation who will bring to the earth things that no other generation brought. Songs, ideas, projects, words, and sounds. This is a characteristic of the sons and daughters of intimacy. But for this to be seen in our lives, we must overcome the temptation to look like others. The most glorious things of God are activated in the risk zone, when we are willing to be who God created us to be, regardless of the price. *Jacob did not fit the clothes of Esau, David did not fit the armor of Saul, and you will never be comfortable dressed like someone you were not created to be.*

Human Obsessions

Notice how Jacob acted according to his identity. He had been defined, and his actions corresponded to who he thought he was. The story endures. It was all deception and effort to obtain blessings. Nothing was flowing out. God had extraordinary plans for him, yet he lived as a slave. He already had the blessing of his brother and father. Now, his obsession was a woman. He believed that if he finally got that woman he loved so much, he would be complete. He worked seven years for her. He was cheated. At this point, I believe that many are identifying themselves with Jacob. After fourteen years of struggles, extra human efforts, and amorous disappointments, he finally got his prize—Rebekah. Someone might say that now Jacob would be satisfied. However, we notice that it wasn't so. There was something locked inside of him that did not allow him to enjoy any of these achievements. Once he obtained the woman he always longed for, he became obstinate with cattle (representing material goods and money). He fooled his father-in-law to get the best offspring. It's amazing to see the strategy Jacob used this time (if you do not know it, I encourage you to read it in your Bible). I am amazed of what a person is able to do in order to get a material "blessing." He got the best sheep. He had everything he longed for, yet he lived the following days of his life running away. He could not enjoy anything he had achieved. Just as in the story of the beginning, God saw him as a chosen one, but he could not see himself like that. Something had happened that did not allow him to understand how God saw him. He had reached his greatest ambitions, but he was far from the desires that God had for Him. We note that he lived all his life with a hunger within him unable to be satisfied with any fruit of this world. This chronic seeker of blessing, obsessed with the approval of others, and compulsively dissatisfied, was about to have an experience with God that would forever transform his life and that of his generations.

The Day When Everything Changed

God visited him one night, and the next morning Jacob was not the same. *It takes Satan a lifetime to corrupt someone's identity, but it takes God only one night to restore it.* The potential that a true encounter with the Living God has to transform years of frustration into a new path of fulfillment, is tremendous.

Jacob was so accustomed to fighting for everything that he fought until dawn with his Creator. Finally, he demanded the blessing that neither his brother, nor his father, nor his wife, nor the money had been able to give him. God touched his thigh and blessed him. He felt the touch and gaze of his Eternal Father. God changed his way of walking and his name. He had never replied to a name other than "deceiver." For the first time, he heard a Being full of an unknown love calling him in a different and supreme way: Israel, "he who fights with God" (not against God, as many translate it). God redefined and redirected him. It affected his life and his generations in such a way that until today the nation chosen by God honors and responds to that name with which God named him that night. I think we have no dimension of what happens when the Father of love redefines us. Not only our life and our walk is affected, but also generations and nations are favored by that divine instant. Finally, Jacob was satiated. *"So Jacob called the name of the place Peniel, saying, 'For I have seen God face to face, and yet my life has been delivered.'"*[18]

But my question is: What was the bond that so affected Jacob, which God released that night? What circumstance had defined him in such a way as to live his whole life running away, deceiving, and seeking the favor of men? Had it been just the name his parents had given him? A few years ago I began to pray and present these questions to the Holy Spirit. Something had defined Jacob and I needed to find it out. God took me to the beginning of this story and taught me two principles that transformed my life. The first one is found in Genesis 25:28, NKJV:

> ***"And Isaac loved Esau*** *because he ate of his game, but Rebekah loved Jacob."*
> Emphasis added by the author

Jacob lacked paternal love. Jacob did not feel loved by his father. That experience defined him. Jacob always sought the love of his father but he did not obtain it from him. The panorama began to clear before my eyes. Only a person who does not feel valued by their father can act this way. This is the spirit of religiosity. It introduces orphanhood in such a way that we cannot perceive Abba's love. It is the reason we seek in human systems, and in inferior pleasures to satisfy our desire to be loved by the Father. When we receive the revelation of God's fatherhood and how much He loves us, our identity is redefined. This supreme love becomes the fuel that leads our being towards His will. We no longer seek to satisfy our inner desire with the blessing of men, with the approval of people, with sentimental relationships or with material goods. We can enjoy all these things, because our being is satiated in Him.

The second principle I received is found in Genesis 27:1, NASB:

"Now it came about, when Isaac was old and his eyes
were too dim to see, that he called his older son Esau and
said to him, «My son.»And he said to him, «Here I am.»"
Emphasis added by the author

Jacob did not feel he was seen by his father. Isaac was blind and could not see him. A person who does not feel loved or seen by his father will walk his entire life with an affected and corrupted identity. He will try to see the eyes of others, because there is a need for meaning and relevance in his life, unable to be satisfied by a sight other than the paternal. The essence of religiosity is based on how we act in the eyes of people. We can have sinful lives, but as long as others look at us with approval, we believe that we achieve favor. This is a great deception and a tremendous lie. The eyes of God are fixed on us day and night; in public and in private. Knowing that we are seen by Him gives meaning to everything we do. How many sins would we avoid committing if we were aware of the permanent gaze that God puts on us? We do not need the attention of anyone else, because we have the interest of the most wonderful and relevant Being of eternity. This is why Jacob exclaimed: *"I have seen God face to face, and yet my life has been delivered."* Suddenly, he entered the reality that God was watching him. We are free when we know Dad pays attention to us. He watches us carefully, without losing sight of us for any second. Everything we do is relevant to Him. *The ties of orphanhood rot away when we understand the truth that the Father does not take off His eyes from us despite our mistakes and flights.* In this very moment, as you read these pages, He is contemplating you. As a parent I understand this so well. My gaze is fixed on my little girl. She plays, walks, moves, and I follow her. Although she does not notice it, my eyes are continually drawn to her. I look at her even when she sleeps. In her slightest need my arms of love will be there to help her.

I long for this truth to redefine you. You are loved and seen by the Father. This reality will bring a new spiritual dimension of freedom into your life. You can walk safely and confidently. You will not need the favor of man, nor the pleasures of this world to quench the hunger inside of you. Only His love and His gaze satisfy us. This revelation will determine your life and will affect your generations.

Nathanael, Seen and Loved by Jesus

There are two people in the Bible to whom God reveals the vision of a ladder to Heaven and where the angels of God were ascending and descending on it. The first is Jacob, the second is Nathanael. There is a connection between these two lives and what we have seen so far.

"Philip found Nathanael and said to him, «We have found Him of whom Moses in the law, and also the prophets, wrote—Jesus of Nazareth, the son of Joseph.» And Nathanael said to him, «Can anything good come out of Nazareth?» Philip said to him, «Come and see.» Jesus saw Nathanael coming toward Him, and said of him, «Behold, an Israelite indeed, in whom is no deceit!» Nathanael said to Him, «How do You know me?» Jesus answered and said to him, «Before Philip called you, when you were under the fig tree, I saw you.»"

John 1:45-48, NKJV

Notice, at first, the disbelief of Nathanael before the good news of Philip. This man is clearly frustrated. He responds as an orphan of soul. Philip tells him that they have found He whom they were looking for and the "ironic" Nathanael answers: *"Can anything good come out of Nazareth?"* For out of the abundance of his heart, the mouth speaks, and for this we can know a little of what is happening inside of him. In spite of this, he decides to go to meet Jesus. When He sees him, He defines him with his heavenly identity: *"Behold, an Israelite indeed, in whom is no deceit!"* We do not know much about Nathanael life before this episode, but he was surely on God's agenda for the coming revival, he would become one of His disciples, and later he would be one of the twelve apostles of the early Church. For some, perhaps this man was the "unbeliever" or the "ironic." But for the Father, he was a key to everything that was going to happen on earth. Faithful to his distorted identity, the answering Nathanael replies: *"How do You know me?"* Clearly these words did not have a friendly tone. Jesus' loving gaze and His words of appreciation were something that Nathanael was not accustomed to receiving. His orphaned, religious, and resentful heart did not produce confidence in what he was hearing, but everything is about to change. Suddenly, Jesus says, *"When you were under the fig tree, I saw you."* I would like to emphasize these last words: I saw you.

Certainly something is released inside Nathanael. Suddenly, a fresh revelation floods his understanding. *"Rabbi, You are the Son of God! You are the King of Israel!"* Is not this the same man who just a moment ago was making fun of Him? He is now consumed by the discovery that the Messiah, for whom he has waited for years, stands before him. What has transformed the "unbeliever" and "bitter" religious man into a passionate disciple of Jesus? Knowing that Jesus' eyes were on him when no one else saw him. The message was clear: *Nathanael, you are important to me. When you were under the fig tree and you thought you were alone. When in your frustrated heart you wondered why nobody sees what you do or nobody cares what you say, my eyes of love were fixed on you and for me you are a true worshiper without deception. No matter if you do not feel valued by others, for me you are special and unique. Did you feel that nobody saw you? I saw you when no one else was paying attention to you. And I see you as a key person for what will happen in the next few years in Israel and the nations. I count on you.* Can you see the connection with Jacob? If you still can't see it, I'll give you more revelation to understand. As the next step God gives him the same revelation as the son of Isaac.

> *"Jesus answered and said to him, «Because I said to you, 'I saw you under the fig tree,' do you believe? You will see greater things than these.» And He said to him, «Most assuredly, I say to you, hereafter you shall see heaven open, and the angels of God ascending and descending upon the Son of Man.»"*
> **John 1:50-51, NKJV**

To all those who have been defined by some negative experience in their life, and who are frustrated, unbelieving, dissatisfied, and looking for favor in religion, God presents them a ladder to Heaven. It's an invitation to go up to another level, to a place where you are no longer defined by what the earth says about you but by your eternal identity. What Heaven says about you will shout so loud that it will silence any voice of cursing and religiosity that has tried to corrupt your original design and divine essence. The two points are getting connected, Jacob and Nathanael, they did not feel seen, God showed a stairway to Heaven to both. But, there is still one more important fact. When we search in a Bible dictionary about Nathanael, we find that in John's gospel is the only place where he is called by this name. The other gospels recount the episode by naming him as he who accompanies Philip, Bartholomew. In the book of Acts, he is also called Bartholomew. It's evident that Nathanael and Bartholomew are the same person. But John, who is the intimate disciple, always brings data and details that other gospels do not mention (Could it be that the intimate ones see things that others do not see?). Why does John, who is always close to Jesus, record Bartholomew as Nathanael? Why did Jesus call this man whom everyone else calls Bartholomew, Nathanael? We find the answer when we discover the meaning of each name. Bartholomew means "son of Ptolemy." Nathanael means "gift from God." To all the world this man is the "son of somebody," but Jesus redefines him as "gift from God." His family, his friends, and the very religious system had defined this man with irrelevance, as one more man. I understand a little, now, why his heart showed frustration, disbelief, and apathy. However, he is redefined by God. In other words, Jesus says to him: *I see you, I love you, and you are a gift from God to the earth, and from this day on you will reach spiritual levels that you have never dreamed of in your life.* Just as

Jacob, Nathanael is restored and redirected. God nullified the power of the experiences and definitions that had operated upon them to unleash orphanhood. He revealed Himself as a Father of love and released their fate of glory that would affect generations.

Today you need to be redefined by the voice of the Father. I do not know what experience has marked you so much as to make you an orphan of soul. Perhaps all you long for is to be seen and loved. Today I want to tell you that God has inspired me to write this book just for you. For you to know that Dad's eyes of love cannot get away from you; that His intense and furious love pierce every wall that has been lifted for years around you. He is about to show you a ladder to a new dimension. Your prophetic and glorious destiny is being unleashed now. I do not know who you are for everybody else, but I want to encourage you to take a few minutes and listen to what Jesus thinks of you. Silence every voice and let His Spirit shout within you: *You are my beloved child, you give me pleasure, I see you, I love you, and I have placed a Heavenly ladder before you to gain a new level of love, revelation, and activation because you are a key to everything that is coming. Today you must choose between whatever has tried to define you, and my voice upon you. You are a gift from Heaven to the earth, your generations will be affected if you receive my love. I cannot take my eyes off you. I am your eternal Father, and you are the child of my intimacy.*

PRACTICAL GUIDE CHAPTER 6

· *Seen and Loved by the Father* ·

Questions to share in groups, cells or leadership teams:

1. What are the experiences that have marked you in life and have defined your character, relationships and purpose?

2. What are the desires and longings you pursue in your life? Is there a relationship between them and the circumstances that marked you in your childhood or adolescence?

3. Do you recognize moments in which God came to encounter you to redefine you or to redeem corrupted areas of your life? Describe some of them.

4. What difference do you find between the ways people have seen you and how God sees you? Declare in the group how God sees you and how He calls you.

Personal application exercise:

I would like you to make a list of the circumstances that have marked and defined you in life. Next, I encourage you to say a prayer of surrender of those moments, asking the Father to redefine you and reveal who you are according to His heart. I declare that as you do so, you will feel the Father's gaze that frees you, and His voice that redefines you.

Circumstance	Prayer

CHAPTER 7

· Going from Slaves to Children – Part I ·

It is not easy to move from a slave to an heir mindset. It is not easy to live as an heir when you have an enemy who always wants you to become a slave again.

They do not follow the signs, but the Father's heart, and then the signs follow them.

Being in the Father's house is not to attend a temple, but to abide in His love. Many serve in the temple but live far away from His love.

CHAPTER 7

· *Going from Slaves to Children – Part I* ·

When God chooses a life and designs a purpose for her, there is absolutely nothing in the universe that can stop the Father's plans. God chose Romina from her mother's womb, although her biological parents did not think so. Within only few days of birth, she was abandoned and then delivered for adoption. Her fate of misfortune was doomed. However, God's grace intervened. She was adopted and raised in a family full of love, acceptance, and care. The love of God changed the inheritance, context, and future of this princess. The Father's plans were higher, and His desires of love for her were clearly intense. Her adoptive parents, being a Christian family, led the little one on the eternal paths. The love in her home was so alive that she never even questioned that she was not born there. However, at teenage, her mother decided she should tell her the truth. So, she told her she was adopted. Although the young woman did not doubt the love of her parents from the heart, the following years brought many questions about her identity and value. It was a fierce war against all the thoughts that tried to move her from the place of divine honor where God had placed her. *It is not easy to move from a slave to an heir mindset. It is not easy to live as an heir when you have an enemy who always wants you to become a slave again.* Although God had changed her identity, her spiritual clothing, inheritance, and destiny, Satan invested his resources to tie her up to a past that God had already redeemed with His grace. The father of lies is adept at distorting identities and perverting inheritances.

Romina's war has been equal to that of hundreds of God's children, who, although they are in the Father's house, they live as slaves. There's a number of prodigal sons and daughters even within the Church itself. There are many adopted by inexhaustible Love, who were introduced to a new home and released to a fate of glory, who are tempted to return again and again to the place from where God has rescued them. God granted me the honor of having Romina as a spiritual daughter. She managed to conquer that battle. Today she is a 28 year old woman, who is establishing a wonderful family, married to Tomás, a great man and minister of God. She has a tremendous youth restoration ministry. I have seen her bring many women to the Lord and be a part of their healing. She has her own shoe company, she honors God with it, and she is a great testimony for each person who comes into that place. It moves me to think of her and imagine the Father's smile when He looks at her. I can observe what God has done all these years and I understand that although it's not easy, when we take the provision of love Abba gives us and live in that divine identity, He can build a life full of favor and purpose. Sometimes we believe that being a prodigal, slave, or spiritual orphan means not attending a church, but it's much more than that. It's not living according to the adoption and inheritance that was entrusted to us. Prodigal means "spendthrift, spender, he who wastes his inheritance in useless ends." What are you doing with the love, forgiveness, grace, favor, and inheritance the Father gave you? If you are not using all those things to do what it was given for you to do, you qualify for the prodigal category. There is a great difference between being a child of God and living as such. Many are sons and daughters, but they live as slaves. They have been adopted, but still live as orphans. They are heirs but they live oppressed by a system that overpowers them. This is the description of religiosity, it's not living in coherence with who we are. You must reflect whether you are living according to who you are and what the Father has provided for you or not. We will analyze the symptoms of a slave's mindset and those of a son's mindset. I am convinced that the same Father who rescued Romina from a life condemned to misery and made her a princess inheriting the Unmovable Kingdom, will do the same with you.

A Servant Mindset

Men were too far away and God decided to send Jesus. The Lamb of God is the expression of a Creator who wants to draw us closer. He models a relationship of intimacy with the Father and guides His beloved ones along this path of closeness. He sits at the table of sinners, washes the feet of His disciples, visits houses, hugs the lepers, approaches the prostitutes, and spends time with the children. That is Emmanuel, God with us. He calls us sons and daughters, He presents Himself as the Bridegroom of the Church and He prefers His disciples to identify themselves with a relationship of friendship with Him, rather than with that of servitude.

"No longer do I call you servants, for a servant does not know what his master is doing; but I have called you friends, for all things that I heard from My Father I have made known to you."

John 15:15, NKJV

Jesus does not contradict His teachings as to having attitudes of service, yet when He speaks on identity, He wants to call us friends. The servant is a slave and has a master. He owes him responsibility and discipline, and if he does not serve him he will be discarded. You cannot get too close to your employer. You just have to do the job and leave on time. He competes when another servant has a better reputation before his master and fears losing his place. He is not an heir. He does not even have a place in his master's house. Jesus makes it clear that it's not the way God wants to relate to His own ones. I understand the concept of serving God, and we know that this is the legacy that Jesus left us; however, I think we have emphasized this function more than the intimacy the Master wants to bring the disciples into. In every nation where I travel, I am greeted with a strong, *Welcome, Servant.* Sometimes I wonder why they call me that, if Jesus calls me friend. I understand what they are referring to and I am clearly there to serve them with humility and love. It is completely biblical, we are servants of God, but if we have to use the biblical emphasis, God calls us sons many more times than servants. To be a son is the title the Father gave me. To be a servant-son will be my testimony when they see my surrender out of love to those the Father has given me. Anyway, I do not want us to reflect on a term, but on something much deeper than this. Are we living as slaves or as sons? In the concept I want to convey, slave, servant, and orphan are synonyms. I mean what someone with that condition was in the time of Jesus. Someone deprived of freedom, without rights, and without intimacy with their master. Someone with no inheritance and predestined to a life of misfortune and suffering. Jesus came to rescue us from that place, to sit us with Christ in the Heavenly places, and to make us joint-heirs with His Kingdom. I would like us to observe some symptoms of the slaves and the sons.

Slaves or Sons?

"Now I say, as long as the heir is a child, he does not differ at all from a slave although he is owner of everything."
Galatians 4:1, NASB

"And because you are sons, God has sent forth the Spirit of His Son into your hearts, crying out, «Abba, Father!» Therefore you are no longer a slave but a son, and if a son, then an heir of God through Christ."
Galatians 4:6-7, NKJV

These are some most revealing verses. Paul describes children who, by their immaturity, live as slaves. They own everything, they were clothed with power and authority, but do not walk coherently with their identity. One of the Holy Spirit's functions is to get you out of bondage and restore both your identity and mindset as a son or daughter. There is a voice shouting from the depths of your being that says: *You are no longer a slave but a son and heir.*

For over ten years I have developed a passion for discipleship. I have trained hundreds of people and collaborated with the process of transforming many "slaves" into "heirs." In our ministry, thousands of these people have come from many churches to be trained for God's work. I have traveled around different nations seeing many sons and daughters in the churches who live as orphans. What I want to share now is just a little of what I have learned along the way. This has been my conclusion in all these years of observing young people, pastors, leaders, musicians, great ministers, and people who are starting on the path of the Kingdom. In the following chapters I will share a comparative picture between someone with a slave's/orphan's mindset and someone with a son's mentality. If you identify with the descriptions in the first column, I want to show you the new and living way that Jesus has opened to go back to the Father's house.

1. The Main Symptom

Orphan's/ Slave's Midset		Son's Mindset
Operates out of fear	**Main Symptom**	Operates out of love

"For you have not received a spirit of slavery leading to fear again, but you have received a spirit of adoption as sons by which we cry out, «Abba! Father!» The Spirit Himself testifies with our spirit that we are children of God."

Romans 8:15-16, NASB

Paul teaches the Romans that fear is a symptom of one who has a spirit of a slave. He lives in fear of everything. He fears being rejected, condemned, and discarded. He is afraid to make decisions, and fears the future. The employee is always afraid his boss will fire him. He does not feel secure and, at some point, he has uncertainty about the future. Those who have a slave's mindset live full of insecurity and distrust. In Jesus' time, the slave had to operate out of fear of his masters. He could not get close to them. The Bible teaches us about the fear of God, it says that it guides us to wisdom and to closeness to Him. However, fear distances you from God. Do you want to identify someone who operates as an orphan? He does not trust anyone. He always thinks that something bad is going to happen to him. He lives in fear and feels rejected by God. There are thousands of stories of orphaned children who, because of their bad experiences, when they arrive at a house where they are received with sincere love, distrust the kindness and escape at night to continue their path of misfortune.

I remember I was arriving to minister in another nation in Latin America. A chauffeur they had hired came to pick me up. It took me just a few minutes of being with him and seeing the expression on his face to realize that he did not live as a child of God. On my way to my destination, he told me he was an Arab and a very religious man. I asked him the question, *How is your relationship with God?* He replied, *I am afraid of God, that's why I keep everything that the Scriptures say.* His face and voice revealed a bitter man. He was a slave, and God was distant and repressive to him. His heart felt like a block of impenetrable cement. However, God gave me the key to take him to the Father's house. I began to ask him about his family. He told me he had a daughter he loved with all his heart. I asked him what he loved most about his daughter. He told me that when she was a girl he loved her hugs and when she called him "daddy." Now she had grown up, yet those moments in which she expressed that spontaneous and passionate love were his delight. My questions followed: *Would you like her to be afraid of you?* He looked at me with a pensive face, and responded by moving his head to both sides expressing a clear negative. Then I said to him: *God calls you son. He sent Jesus, and Jesus sent His Spirit of adoption so that we no longer have fear, and so now we can call Him Daddy. Just as you delight in the love of your daughter, He delights in your love.* This experience ended up with the man accepting Jesus as his eternal Father and going from slave to son. It's wonderful to see the Spirit of adoption in action!

He who has been restored in the son's mindset operates out of love. He trusts and unleashes faith in every circumstance. The son knows there's nothing that can get him out of the Father's house. The inexhaustible love of the Father flows unstopping like an impetuous river. No matter what may happen, in any circumstance he can count on the help of his Father. He will never be alone. His future is in the hands of Someone higher. As long as he does not let go of His hand, the fate of glory will be assured. Even if his natural parents abandon him, God will take him. He who lives as a son lives confidently, feels loved, and has no fears. *He who has been perfected in love no longer fears.*[19]

2. Identity

Orphan's/ Slave's Midset		Son's Midset
Based in **doing**	Idetity	Based in **being**

"And the devil said to Him, «If You are the Son of God,
tell this stone to become bread.»"

Luke 4:3, NASB

The slave feels that if he does not do something he has no value. His esteem is on doing and in feeling approved by his boss. The value of a child is not in what he does but in who he is. It is better to allow the Father defining us or surely someone else will. That is why, when Jesus was affirmed in His identity as Son, Satan, in the desert, tempted Him by trying to take Him from "being" to "doing:" *If you are a son, turn the stone into bread.* In other words, *If you are a son, I want to see ademonstration of power.* The slave needs to demonstrate power to feel he is valued. If his preaching does not appear to be super-anointed, if he does not have many gifts, if he does not seem to have been endowed with great talents, or if he does not pray as many hours as the great men of God say, he feels he is not worthy. The voice of religion continues to say to the sons and daughters: *If you do not turn stones into bread, or if you do not fly with the angels, you are not a child of God.* Many are pressed to fulfill demands that Satan is imposing upon them (although these are disguised as pious things), and without realizing it they end up prostrate before him. The motivation of Jesus' ministry was not the demonstration of power, but the obedience to the Father. Jesus does not expose His power to the demands of the religious system nor Satan. He tells them about intimacy with and dependence on the Father. And, when the flashes of the Pharisees' cameras are switched off, He suddenly feeds thousands of hungry ones with two loaves and five fish. We build ministries of power on the basis of our intimacy with the Father. To be a slave, you have to do something. If you don't, you will be fired and rejected. On the other hand, the son operates from the truth that he is loved and accepted by the Father, and nothing and no one can change this reality. The orphan always feels that he is being tested, but the son accepts the irreversible approval Jesus gave him on the cross of Calvary. Those who have a slave mindset base their identity on gifts, talents, and even in their service to God, but service must flow from our identity as sons and daughters. That was the order God has established in Jesus. The system preaches: *You are valuable because of what you do.* Heaven declares, *You are valuable because of who you are.* God builds powerful and transcendent ministries in those who have understood that before being super-Christians, they are children of God. To be a son or daughter you have to know who you are to the Father and cultivate your relationship with Him. Your value is in what God thinks and declares of you, and nothing can make you feel less than that. The problem with those who operate as slaves is that on the day their preaching did not seem to be so anointed, or the person for whom they prayed was not healed or the worship did not flow as they wanted, they become depressed and feel that God no longer loves them.

Each year, we receive hundreds of students who come to the MiSion Ministerial Training Center to be trained for ministry. In the first interviews they spend hours detailing their ministries, describing their gifts, and how much God uses them. Many fill the minutes talking about ministerial work, but very few tell us about their relationship with the Father. In seconds, we can identify if the person is operating from an orphaned place, since they need to establish their valuation in achievements and capacities more than in what the Father says of them. They love the platform more than the Father's lap, and when we search their heart we see that they are full of fears, envy, and dissatisfaction. However, after a process, we observe how God transforms them into a generation that rather than turning stones into bread, they feed on the words of the Father and they only respond to His voice. These will be like Jesus, the spiritual parents of the glorious Church Christ is building in the nations. *They do not follow the signs, but the Father's heart, and then the signs follow them.* I deeply believe that our spiritual curricula will no longer be needed for us to be valued by the religious system. In many meetings I attend, if I do not say that I travel around the nations, that I preach to thousands of people, and that I write books, it seems that I am not valuable. When someone introduces me or presents me to others, he tells them about my accomplishments, and people change their attitude towards me. Why should it be so? I believe in a generation of children of God who will value others for what they are, because of their hearts, for what the Father says about them. Those who write books and whose faces appear in the posters for conferences will be equally honored and valued as those who—in the anonymity of their places—cry and obey the Father in the darkness of the corners of each city. We will not be a kingdom where artists, singers, super-pastors, or charismatic ones are more valuable than the rest, but where the obedient sons and daughters of God will be valued, and then the earth will see their manifestation. Never again put your confidence in your abilities or in what others say about you. Your value is what cost God to give His Only Son to die on the cross out of love for you. Remember, you are worthy of what the Father says about you. You need nothing more than to listen to His voice on this day and to know that He delights Himself when He thinks of you.

3. Self-Image

Orphan's/ Slave's Midset		Son's Mindset
Insecurity, comparison to others, low self-esteem, self-rejection, and a continuos sense of condemnation	Self-Image	Secure in the love of the Father, full of appreciation and affirmation for this relationship with God. He feels unique and loved

"For God does not show favoritism."

Romans 2:11, NLT

At this point, you have already realized that the spirit of slavery, or orphanhood, or prodigal son, are spiritual synonyms. All of them operate by taking the children out of the place the Father has imagined for them. The three of them, orphan, slave, and prodigal, act from fear, insecurity, low self-esteem, and continuous condemnation. The slave always believes that someone will take his place from him. He lives in constant competition, jealousy, and comparison. He feels insecure. Because his security is set on doing, it becomes a circumstantial trust. When things go well, he feels loved by God. But as soon as he faces an error or problem, he feels that God does not love him as much. Thus, he becomes a double-minded man and, therefore, as the Word says, he is unstable in all his ways.[20] Sometimes he feels like a superman, and other times he is the worst of them all. This is what a slavery's mindset produces. On the other hand, he who lives with a son's mindset is constant in the love of the Father. As the love of God does not grow nor decrease for us, because God is Love, if we abide in His love, we live in confidence. Jesus said, *"Just as the Father has loved Me, I have also loved you."*[21] Can you imagine how much the Father loves Jesus? Can you understand how much Jesus loves you? Even in the face of adversity, a son knows that all things will be for his good, because God is in control. The furious love of God overcomes all orphanhood, and it can make the one whom the world has despised feel complete. Each child is unique and special to the Father. As a great friend says: *God has no favorites, He has intimates.* And they are those who abide in His love and enjoy His joy. Sometimes God uses us a lot, and sometimes He seems not to use us as much, but His love does not change. We have weeks where we pray all day long, and we have weeks where we fight all day long, but His love does not change. When we are strong, when we are weak, His love does not change. Good seasons, bad seasons, dark winters, sunny summers, nothing can alter the love of the One who loves us with eternal love. We can walk safely, we can serve the Kingdom with total confidence, and minister from the very basis that God has approved us by His love, and we know that from Dad's hand there will always be new dawns full of grace and favor. The goodness and the mercy of God pursue His sons and daughters every day of their lives. As you can see, the way back to the Father's house is open. You do not have to make any effort, He has already made it. You need to go back. I'm not talking about you leaving the church. *Being in the Father's house is not to attend a temple, but to abide in His love.* Many serve in the temple, but live far away from His love. It is the Kingdom of God on earth. There is a unique place for you. He is waiting for you with open arms to tell you that you are no longer a slave, but a son; and if a son, then an heir. I encourage you to advance a little further on this wonderful road. In the next chapter, we will describe some more aspects to remove all spirit of slavery and live in the fullness that Abba provides.

PRACTICAL GUIDE CHAPTER 7

· *Going from Slaves to Children – Part I* ·

Questions to share in groups, cells or leadership teams:

1. Is it possible that there are prodigal children within the Church? Why do you think there are many who attend worship each week, but do not live as children of God?

2. What symptoms do we identify in Christians who see themselves only as servants of God and have not had the revelation of God's paternity?

3. Why are so many of God's children living in fear today? What are the consequences of a Christian who operates out of fear?

4. What are the problems we find in the children of God when they emphasize doing over being?

Personal application exercise:

Mark with an (X) in the following areas if you feel identified with the orphan/slave mindset or son mindset, according to what you read in the chapter. At the end, write a commitment of practical actions to go from slave to son in the necessary areas.

Orphan's/ Slave's Midset		Son's Mindset
	Main Symptom	
	Identity	
	Self-Image	

CHAPTER 8

· *Going from Slaves to Heirs – Part II* ·

*For religious persons, sin
affects their ministry and
the image they have built
before men. For intimate
ones, sin contaminates the
delight of their relationship
with the Father.*

*Loving is more powerful
than judging when we want
to transform.*

*Each person is a by-product
of how she prays.*

CHAPTER 8

· *Going from Slaves to Heirs – Part II* ·

4. Ministerial Motivations

Orphan's/ Slave's Midset		Son's Mindset
Wants to win the favor or acceptance of others. Constant desire to please men. Vain-glories (fame, money, reputation)	**Ministerial Motivations**	Finds pleasure and delight in doing the Father's will. Constant desire to please the Father. Eternal glory even if he or she loses fame, money, reputation

"...and [I am] also a partaker of the glory that will be revealed."

1 Peter 5:1, NKJV

He who has an orphan's mindset feels so insecure that he seeks his value in the approval of others, or in ministerial success. The motivation for spiritual service is selfish. He does not think of others, but only himself and how to grow in reputation. He lives to do what men like and to give them what they ask for. The goals of their service are fame, money, and recognition, although they commonly express the opposite with their mouths. They look for contacts, and they open doors by force, they do "lobbying" and "spiritual politics." Their minds are set in temporary success and away from the supreme Model.

Sons and daughters just want to please and obey the Father. They delight in fulfilling the will of God even if they end up beheaded or nailed to a cross. They have an insatiable desire to see Jesus smile, even if on the way to achieve it they lose money, reputation, fame, and favor of men. They have been free from vain glories and they are consumed by eternal glory. Their ministerial motivation is anchored in eternity. Peter made it clear. He said his whole ministry had a motivation: *"Being a partaker of the glory that will be revealed."* In God's eternal script there will be a moment of climax called the manifestation of the glory to come. Suddenly, the curtains of Heaven will open, and Jesus will manifest Himself in the clouds. So, for you to have an understanding of the glory that will emanate from the person of Jesus, let me show you how Isaiah describes it:

> *"Then the moon will be abashed and the sun ashamed,*
> *for the Lord of hosts will reign on Mount Zion and in*
> *Jerusalem, and His glory will be before His elders."*
> **Isaiah 24:23, NASB**

His glory will be so powerful that the moon will be ashamed, and His light will be so bright that the sun will be confused. On sunny days, when the morning star shines brightly, I love to look at it and say, *You're going to be confused, when Jesus returns.* On full moon nights, when it illuminates the seas and the earth, I like to observe it and remind it of the Word of God: *"You will be ashamed when the beauty of Jesus is revealed."*

It will be the culminating moment of God's work and the beginning of what is really worth for eternity. And Peter said, *I live and serve for that day, there is nothing in this world that can be compared to the glory that will be revealed.* The success of a man is not measured by the greatness of his earthly ministry, but by the dimension of the Kingdom he represents.

Sons and daughters have their sight set on the supreme award. That is their highest goal. That is their ministerial motivation. Slaves want to be recognized by men. Sons know that small acts of obedience give them greatness in the coming Kingdom.[22] At this point I must ask: Are you living as a son/daughter or as a slave?

5. Motivation for Holiness

Orphan's/ Slave's Midset	Motivation to Live in Holiness	Son's Mindset
Avoids rejection of God. Legalism. Comply with the rules not to be rejected		Enjoys intimacy with the Father without contamination. Holiness out of love

"Your people shall be volunteers in the day of Your power; in the beauties of holiness."

Psalm 110:3, NKJV

The slave operates by discipline. He has to comply with rules and schedules. The son works by delight. He only wants to please the Father. Spiritual slaves within the church seek holiness only to fulfill the law, not to honor the Giver of it. The orphan keeps church schedules. He does not want to go to worship but when it's time he knows he has to show up. He does everything by obligation. He seeks holiness so his boss does not fire and reject him.

On the other hand, the son operates by delight. *"I was glad when they said to me, «Let us go into the house of the Lord,»"* declared the "son" David.[23] It is proven that love is a far more powerful motivator than doing things by discipline. The son and the wife, are much more effective than the servant and the slave. God's children know that sin contaminates the relationship of love with God. They seek holiness because they can't imagine the idea of not feeling the embrace of the Father, or seeing the Spirit become saddened. This is called holiness out of love. When the "slave" Saul sinned, he only cared about maintaining his reputation and ministry, so he lied to Samuel. He was more interested in what men thought than in what God felt.[24] When the "son" David sinned, he said: *"Do not cast me away from Your presence... Restore to me the joy of Your salvation."*[25] *For religious persons, sin affects their ministry and the image they have built before men. For intimate ones, sin contaminates the delight of their relationship with the Father.* I am faithful to my wife not to fulfill a rule, or for her not to divorce me. I am faithful because I long to enjoy the purity of our love and to feel that nothing stands between us. Can you see the difference? God is awakening a generation of sons and daughters who seek holiness in order to enjoy the beauty it imparts, and not losing any of the benefits of the fullness of Christ.

6. Sources of Pleasure and Comfort

Orphan's/ Slave's Midset	Sources of Pleasure and Comfort	Son's Mindset
Looks for pleasure far from God. Addictions, pornography, vices, passions of the flesh, misrepresented relationships		Looks for times of reset in the Presence of God. Desire for the Word, for worship environments, for Kingdom relations

"Come to Me, all who are weary and heavy-laden, and I will give you rest."

Matthew 11:28, NASB

When we are weighed down and tired, sons and daughters go to Jesus. He is the greatest existing place of rest and recreation. However, when slaves finish their religious task, they go over to the other extreme. They are like a family man who works all day long and when he gets home, he does not even want to talk about work. There are many men of God who, after finishing their weekends burdened by church activities, are immersed in porn, infidelities, vices, and pleasures of the flesh on Monday. They have slave's mindset and they find rest away from the Father's house. Sin is a source of comfort to many. The great falls are a consequence of unresolved sadness or roots of bitterness. Many seek to relieve pains of the soul through sinful medicines such as lust, relationships outside of God, sins related to the virtual world and social networks. The list could go on and on for pages. These sources of pleasure only increase tiredness and grief, moving more orphans to isolation, away from the purpose and the arms of Jesus. When we feel we are eating the food of the pigs and perceive our filth, we must run to the Father who is waiting for us. That's what a son does. Fatigue must lead us to the One who can bear our burdens. The sadness of the soul finds relief in Jesus. Surrounding ourselves with environments of worship and atmospheres of the Kingdom are the key to renew our spirit and not fall into the stress slavery proposes. Nurturing ourselves with the Word, which is the greatest medicine, is the key. I believe that the problem is not ecclesiastical activism, but to carry out activities without hearing the Father and without feeling His caress. Stress does not come from the tasks, but from taking our sight off of Jesus. Doing the Father's will must be our food. Food provides us with energy, growth, vitamins, and strength. When we are weak or tired, what strengthens us is obeying God and doing His will. What is His will?

Loving Him with all our strength, and loving our neighbor as we love ourselves. Preaching His Word to the lost, studying the Scriptures, and worshiping Him passionately are places of strength and nurture for the children of God. Jesus goes on to say: *"Come to me."* He is not interested in the condition you are in, after His touch you will not remain the same. Children find solace in the Father. Slaves run away from Him. Do you live as a son or as a slave? The next time you plan a time for rest, do not think only of a place to relax, think of a Person. Go to Jesus and you will find rest.

7. Relationship with Others

Orphan's/ Slave's Midset		Son's Mindset
Competition, criticism, comparison, jealousy, and rivalry	**Relationship with Others**	Honor, humility, dependence, sense of being part of the Body
Accusation and exposure, leaving others in bad position to look good	**Handling Mistakes of Others**	With love, covers, gives mercy and forgiveness, while providing ways for restoration

"Let nothing be done through strife or vainglory; but in lowliness of mind let each esteem other better than themselves."

Philippians 2:3, KJV

The slave lives by comparing himself to others. He always wants what others have. Slaves hurt their backs all the time, and that may be because of their work but they also feel miserable for what Proverbs 14:30 says: *"But envy is rottenness to the bones."* Slaves are always looking at others with jealousy, wanting to have their ministry, their anointing, their goods, and even their wife. They are capable of "killing" to get that. By basing their identity and value on *doing*, they always have to be competing, lest someone come and do more and take their place. They have the Cain syndrome, they are "older brothers" who look at their "younger brothers" with contempt. It does not matter that God is pleased with Abel's offerings. The first murder was made against a *worshiper* (at this point we have understood that worshiper and son are spiritual synonyms). He did not kill an enemy but his own brother. Today in the Church, hundreds of "Cain's" continue to kill those whose offerings are accepted by God. They sacrifice them with criticism, jealousy, accusations, and curses. Like the elder brother of the prodigal son, they do not rejoice with the joy of their neighbor, but they weep at their own sorrows. When this young man saw how the Father of love received the one who had returned with repentance, he said: *"Look! For so many years I have been serving you and I have never neglected a command of yours; and yet you have never given me a young goat, so that I might celebrate with my friends."*[26] Do you notice the symptoms of a slave's mindset? *"For so many years I have been serving you"* (he places his value on doing), *"I have never neglected a command of yours"* (he pursues holiness to avoid rejection), *"you have never given me a young goat"* (he refers to a salary, and not an inheritance, we will see this point below). Jesus, the true model of a big brother and of a son, does not condemn even the adulterous woman to whom everyone wants to throw stones. He honors everyone who comes to Him. He promotes His disciples, elevates them from fishermen to fishers of men, from tax collectors to eternal Kingdom's stewards. The only time He says, *"Learn from Me,"* He is not speaking about His gifts or His powers, but of His character: *"Learn from Me, for I am gentle and humble in heart, and you will find rest for your souls."*[27] How does the slave handle others' mistakes? He exposes and accuses them. He sees the mistakes of others as an opportunity for his own growth. He makes comments like: *I told you, there was something about this person that was not okay, everything comes to light, let him have what he deserves.* On the other hand, children provide paths of restoration. When something is not okay with someone, they will quickly attack the problem, seeking to restore the sinner. They see others' falls as personal losses. We are one Body, if a part of it is hurt, the whole Body feels pain. Judgment will be God's last tool with the earth when He has exhausted all the ways of love. Why then does judgment come first for many, before love? You have authority over what you love. That is why God has authority over the world, because He loved it radically. Do you want to transform your nation? You must love it first. Do you want to transform your generation? You must love it first. Do you want to transform your neighbor? You must love him first. *When we want to transform, loving is more powerful than judging.* The slave is independent and selfish. The son is dependent and generous. The son knows he is unique and loved by the Father. When another child prospers in something he is waiting for, he feels God is trying to inspire him. *If I did it with him, I will do it with you as well. Rejoice with your brother, and he will rejoice with you later.* It is *time* to see others as God sees them. We need more people clothed with forgiveness and mercy: sons and daughters who reflect the Father in honor and love for others.

8. Relationship with Authority

Orphan's/ Slave's Midset		Son's Mindset
Sees authority as a source of pain; without trust; lacks a submissive heart. Takes exhortation as condemnation	Relationship with Authority	Honors, respects. Sees it as the provision of God for personal good. Takes discipline as the key for his or her growth

"But if you are without discipline, of which all have become partakers, then you are illegitimate children and not sons."

Hebrews 12:8, NASB

"The slave does not remain in the house forever; the son does remain forever."

John 8:35, NASB

The slave does not receive the exhortation. He cannot conceive the Father's love behind a reprimand. When he hears it, he feels rejected. The father who loves, disciplines. But his wounded heart does not let him see the love behind the instruction. It is important to understand that authority is a fundamental principle of the Kingdom of God. The Father establishes authorities in all areas. The orphan has no parents. The slave does not have them, either. Those who neither submit nor love authority, are orphans and slaves. Living without discipline is for bastards and not for children. This mentality leads people to independence and self-reliance. Many orphans spiritualize rebellion with the idea that God is the only authority and that spiritual cover is not necessary. Clearly, the purpose for which God has given us tutors in every area of life is lost on them. The slave receives the warning as condemnation. It has happened to me many times when exhorting someone and he feels condemned or rejected. Most likely, it's because he has been injured by authority, whether his natural parents or leaders in some area, and his mind has been enslaved with orphanhood.

At the other extreme, we have children who honor their authorities. They understand that the Voice of God often challenges us, but it guides us to life. *"Reproofs of instruction are the way of life,"* says Proverb 6:23 (NKJV). To love the divine direction is to understand that the Father sees things that we do not see, and that He has put people in place to help us not to make mistakes. My little daughter approaches the plugs without knowing the danger putting her little fingers there entails. Thus, what looks like a small game, can be a way to death. I must shout in a firm voice: *No! Do not go there.* My voice has to sound loud and firm so that she understands the dimension of danger. At the moment, she cries and cries, she does not understand why her father speaks to her like this. She does not have the ability to understand the reason for my rebuke. A two-year-old girl cannot interpret my love behind that reprimand. Can you understand how God works? He sees things we do not see. Loving His rigid voice, or the counsel of a pastor, or the challenge of a father, is to obey even though we often do not understand. Only a child who trusts in the love of his Father can live in this dimension. Discipline is a key to a child's growth. All men of God are tested in this area. Many are not approved and stall. The defining characteristic of a child is their obedience based on love and trust. The slave does not obey, he only works for salary. Fulfilling and obeying are not the same. Fulfillment, has to do with tasks. Obeying, has to do with people. The spiritual orphan is the one who does what the authority or the pastor asks of him. The son is the one who loves authority and loves the pastor beyond what they ask for. The slave submits, the son loves to submit himself and enjoys being under authority. He sees each exhortation as a growth opportunity. Jesus said that the slave does not stay in the house forever, but the son does. One symptom of orphanhood is not staying in the places where God has placed you. Sometimes at the least discomfort, people seek to leave their church. Most of the time this situation is not born in the Voice of the Father, but in the difficulty of passing through processes that have been put by God to invigorate our lives. The sons and daughters of intimacy remain in the house, and in this way they are strengthened to affect and transform the environment.

I encourage you to remove all mentality of slavery. Go now to your spiritual authorities and renew your commitment of love with them. Ask them to tell you every time they see a mistake, tell them that you long to be corrected, that you want to grow. If you need to ask for forgiveness, do not hesitate, it is the attitude that children have with their parents. Brokenness sets the way back to the Father's house.

9. Vision of God and Favorite Words

Orphan's/ Slave's Midset		Son's Mindset
Sees a distant God. Has no issues with the greatness of God. Has difficulties in intimacy	**Vision of God**	Sees a close God. Understands the greatness and glory of his Father, but knows the strength of his/her relationship with Him is based on intimacy
- Use me - I'm your servant - I'm not worthy	**Favorite Words**	- I love You - I'm Your son/ daughter - Abba

"And because you are sons, God has sent forth the Spirit
of His Son into your hearts, crying out, «Abba, Father!»"
Galatians 4:6, NKJV

Few people have problems with God's greatness, but many cannot comprehend His closeness. Even the pagans recognize that God is great. Religious men look at the Heavens and the universe and they are astonished at His omnipotence. It is not necessary to have an intimate relationship with God to recognize His holiness, His power, and His wonders. But only children can call Him Dad. Everyone watches Lionel Messi and marvels at his soccer skills. They can shout at him master, genius, the most powerful of the history of the soccer. They can know his statistics in detail. They do not need to have a relationship with him to do it. However, only his child can call him dad. For everyone else, he is an idol. Slaves see God as a powerful, distant, and intimidating Master. They can know His works and the book of His statistics in detail. However, we can make God an idol when we don't see Him as our Father. Sons and daughters see God as a tender and loving Father. God doesn't stop being powerful, wonderful, omnipotent, and splendid when we recognize He likes to hug us, kiss us, and being called Dad by us.

Your vision of God can help you identify whether you are operating as a slave or as a son. Let's look at the words with which you approach Him. We all yearn to be used by God, but slaves just want to be used. Being a servant is about that, that your master uses you. The slave is exploited. I remember when I only prayed: *Lord, use me!* One day God answered me: *Things are used, people love each other. You are not a thing to me, you are a beloved son.* The son bases his relationship on love, while the servant bases it on utility. If the words that you pray the most are use me instead of I love you Dad, you're in serious trouble. The favorite words of a slave are: *Use me, I am your slave, your useless servant, I am not worthy of anything, I am a vile sinner, just give me your crumbs.* Although all these could be theologically correct prayers in some cases, they have been made to

God in certain specific occasions, in special contexts. For example, being a useless servant is used only once as something positive, and several times as those who will perish in hell. It is interesting to remember how, during my childhood and adolescence, I listened to so many men of God praying and repeating this. By vast majority, in the New Testament we are taught to pray as sons and daughters, as the Lamb's Wife, as friends of Jesus, as beloved disciples. All positions involving commitment to intimacy and eternity. In Paul's letters, the word "slave" is used more than ten times as something negative. It's only mentioned as slaves of Christ, in the context of those who had been called to the Lord by being earthly or free slaves. However, I hear the prayer: "We are your slaves," in hundreds of churches, and I hardly hear people who, when they pray, call God Abba. I say this again, I do not want to argue about terms, but it is important to understand that out of the abundance of the heart the mouth speaks. Do you pray as a slave or as a son? Do you worship as an orphan or as an heir? Do you only sing of the greatness of God or can you worship with expressions that denote your intimacy? I believe that the revolution of the sons and daughters of God will be manifested when the Church begins to see, hear, and speak as children. Imagine my daughter approaching me every morning to tell me: *Dad, I am your useless servant, use me, forgive me, I am not worthy to be your daughter.* I think I would already be depressed. Thank God that He does not go into depression! I understand that at times it is necessary to use some of these words in our dynamics with God; however, I believe that He likes us to use other words. The important thing is that up to this point, you are able to identify how many symptoms of slavery you have, and that you will take a path determined to go to the Father's arms.

10. Reward

Orphan's/ Slave's Midset		Son's Mindset
Salary, temporary remuneration	**Reward**	Inheritance, eternal glory

"Therefore you are no longer a slave but a son, and if a son, then an heir of God through Christ."

Galatians 4:7, NKJV

Slaves demand salary. Children claim inheritance. Wage is a temporary reward, while inheritance is an eternal reward. The slave asks for his own things. He demands of God his well-being, his money, his house, his car, because he only cares about his little personal kingdom. The son expects his inheritance. He doesn't have his eyes set on the benefits of this world, he is anchored in eternal glory. Nothing that this earth offers could quench his inner thirst, since he is predestined to inherit something greater. In Psalm 2, we see Jesus claiming His inheritance: *"I will declare the decree: The Lord has said to Me, «You are My Son, today I have begotten You. Ask of Me, and I will give You the nations for Your inheritance, and the ends of the earth for Your possession.»"* The Son claims what the Father promised—the nations. All the earth and its fullness are God's. An heir is the one who legally owns all the property of his father. What is the Father's, can be claimed by His children.

"Now I say, as long as the heir is a child, he does not differ at all from a slave although he is owner of everything."

Galatians 4:1, NASB

There are many sons who are lords of everything, but because of their immaturity, they live like slaves. They think, walk, and pray like slaves. We need a generation who takes their inheritance. The inheritance of the children is to see this generation bowing down before Jesus, to see the greatest harvest of souls that history has witnessed, to preach the Gospel of the Kingdom in all nations, to see the beauty of the Beloved One filling the whole earth, to rule with our Father in this world for eternity. In my family, we don't pray for our needs. Not because it's not right, it's perfectly biblical to do it, but we have determined in our lives not to ask for wages. Instead, we ask for inheritance. We only pray for great things that have to do with the Kingdom of God. We have learned the principle: *"Seek first the kingdom of God and His righteousness, and all these things shall be added to you."*[28] Whenever we seek for something great, the small things come along, but whenever we look for the small things we lose the big ones. God has blessed us with abundance in every detail, but we have defined that we will not be a family of slaves claiming their monthly salary, but we will live as heirs who ask for the nations for Jesus. My little girl does not demand food, clothes, or even her toys. I take care of her needs. If I can do it, how much more will our Father of love give us exactly what we need? Do you think that it's a coincidence that having such a young age, I have already traveled through many different countries on three continents, preaching Jesus? *Each person is a by-product of how they pray.* It is time to claim your inheritance. You are a son and heir. Now, reject the spirit of slavery within you. Being a spirit, it is not static. It is not enough to understand this message. It is necessary to reject every day that diabolical activity over your life that comes and goes, trying to get you away from the purpose of the Father. Orphanhood is not going away just because you have this book in your hands, nor because you understand the message, not even if you preach it. You can declare a thousand times that you are a son and continue living as an orphan. However, when you begin to spend time with the Father and you are determined to hear His voice daily, you are truly free. Staying firm in freedom is achieved by walking each day in dependence on the Father. Orphanhood can only be extinguished when you spend time with the Father, you hear what He is saying about you and you respond with a sincere heart: *Abba.*

I want to declare that His love will consume all fear. Now, the Spirit of freedom is operating over your life. If you have identified yourself with symptoms of slavery, you should review the list of son's mindset and begin to develop those areas as your priority. This cannot be achieved by human effort, but as a fruit of your intimacy with the Father. You need to run into His arms right now and ask Him to tell you what He feels for you. You must hear His Voice declaring, *You are no longer a slave, you are my son.* Your inheritance is beginning to be activated, you will begin to live for what you were born to. You will be so consumed by the eternal glory and the will of the Father that everything else will lose its value. You will no longer have devotion for discipline, but for delight. He will strengthen your ministry, because He trusts His children. His Presence will become your greatest source of delight and you will experience Jesus, as your highest pleasure. The religious system has just lost a slave and Heaven has gained a son of intimacy with the Father.

Comparative Table "Going from Slaves to Sons"

Orphan's/ Slave's Midset		Son's Mindset
Operates out of fear	**Main Symptom**	Operates out of love
Based in **doing**	**Identity**	Based in being
Insecurity, comparison to others, low self-esteem, self-rejection, and a continuous sense of condemnation	**Self-Image**	Secure in the love of the Father, full of appreciation and affirmation for his relationship with God. He feels unique and loved
Wants to win the favor or acceptance of others. Constant desire to please men. Vain-glories (fame, money, reputation)	**Ministerial Motivations**	Finds pleasure and delight in doing the Father's will. Constant desire to please the Father. Eternal glory even if he or she loses fame, money, reputation
Avoids rejection of God. Legalism. Comply with the rules not to be rejected	**Motivation to Live in Holiness**	Enjoys intimacy with the Father without contamination. Holiness out of love

Looks for pleasure far from God. Addictions, pornography, vices, passions of the flesh, misrepresented relationships	**Sources of Pleasure and Comfort**	Looks for times of rest in the Presence of God. Desire for the Word, for worship environments, for Kingdom relations
Competition, criticism, comparison, jealousy and rivalry	**Relationship with Others**	Honor, humility dependence, sense of being part of the Body
Accusation and exposure, leaving others in bad position to look good	**Handling Mistakes of Others**	With love, covers, gives mercy and forgiveness while providing ways for restoration
Sees authority as a source of pain; without trust; lacks a submissive heart. Takes exhortation as condemnation	**Relationship with Authority**	Honors, respects. Sees it as the provision of God for personal good. Takes discipline as the key for his or her growth
Sees a distant God. Has no issues with the greatness of God. Has difficulties in intimacy	**Vision of God**	Sees a close God. Understands the greatness and glory of his Father, but knows the strength of his/her relationship with Him is based on intimacy
- Use me - I'm your servant - I'm not worthy	**Favorite Words**	- I love You - I'm Your son/ daughter - Abba
Salary, temporary remuneration	**Reward**	Inheritance, eternal glory

PRACTICAL GUIDE CHAPTER 8

· *Going from Slaves to Heirs – Part II* ·

Questions to share in groups, cells or leadership teams:

1. What are the false motivations for ministry that we can identify in people who have an orphan mentality?

2. What attitudes towards others or authority demonstrate spiritual orphanhood in the children of God?

3. Why is it so difficult for Christians to have an intimate relationship with the Father?

4. Which of all the slave/orphan symptoms studied do you identify most clearly in your ecclesiastical culture and in your nation?

5. What practical actions or strategies could we use to combat orphanhood in this generation?

Personal application exercise:

Mark with an (X) in the following areas if you feel identified with the orphan/slave mindset or the son mindset, according to what you read in the chapter.

At the end, write a commitment of practical actions to go from slave to son in the necessary areas.

	Ministerial Motivations	
	Motivation to Live in Holiness	
	Sources of Pleasure and Comfort	
	Relationship with Others	
	Handling Mistakes of Others	
	Relationship with Authority	
	Vision of God	
	Favorite Words	
	Reward	

CHAPTER 9

· Lost in the Father's Business ·

The sons and daughters of intimacy are willing to die to their personal dreams in order to live the desires of the Father.

As friends of the Bridegroom, we cannot make the Bride to fall in love with us. Our greatest purpose is to get the Church to fall in love with Jesus, not with us.

Life is too short to spend it on things that will not strengthen your eternity.

CHAPTER 9

· *Lost in the Father's Business* ·

When I was a little boy I got lost. We were enjoying a beautiful family beach day. I was about five years old. For a minute my parents were careless, and when a candy salesman passed by, I began to follow him disconnecting myself from time and space. The candies were so appealing to me that I just ran after them. My parents started looking for me all over the place. People united in solidarity at the alert that a child had gone astray. When I realized that I had walked away and did not know how to return, I began to cry. Because of my anguish, someone recognized the situation and carried me on their shoulders. In a few minutes, I was seen by my parents who desperately were looking for me. The encounter was beautiful and I learned my lesson: no temporal candy can replace my parents' arms of love.

Today, there are many spiritual children who are lost, seeking after the sweets of this world and they are, as a result, far removed from their area of safety and purpose. The lovely delights of the flesh and the proposals of the system, pull many children away from the Father's arms. However, the Heavens try to draw the attention. God will send one of His messengers to carry you on their shoulders and to place you again in front of the One who has been looking for you with desperate yearning.

When I was seventeen, I was finishing school with outstanding grades. In my first years of high school, I managed to be in the honor roll of an important institution and to be the flag bearer on several occasions. My teachers and principals encouraged me to pursue a university career oriented to the most important sciences given the ease I had for the study. However, at that age I decided to travel to another nation to a Bible and ministerial training institute. The high school principal told my parents that it was a waste for me to focus on religious things because I could be successful in other careers, and not only make a great future for myself, but also contribute to others. However, from a young age, I got lost and strayed away from the opportunities of the world, but into the will of Heaven. I could not establish a humanly secure future, but a glorious eternity. When we accept the Father's wishes for our lives above the offerings of men, we discover a higher pleasure that this world cannot manufacture. The sweets they offer to us are attractive, and we often leave the places of eternal purposes looking for temporary bowls of lentils. Days before he was killed, Dr. Martin Luther King said: "I am just like everyone else, I want to have a long and happy life. But today, I will not focus on what I want, I will concentrate on what God wants. I may not live the sunny days that remain ahead, but as long as there is light at the end of the road for others, it will be worth for me." *The sons and daughters of intimacy are willing to die to their personal dreams in order to live the desires of the Father.*

Let me share one more story. I had accepted an invitation to go to minister in the Middle East and Israel. A few weeks later, for the first time in years, bombs were falling nearby Jerusalem. When I asked the church to pray for my journey, a sister came to tell me that it was crazy to travel in the midst of such a war, to that war zone. God had given me a word to make the trip, but now that directive was being tested. As if this were not enough, days before traveling we received the wonderful news that we would have a baby. Voices of confusion flooded my mind: *Who would take care of your wife and baby if something happened to you? Wait for another time to travel, there will be more opportunities.* However, the voice of my mind's Creator had been clear and when God speaks there is only one possible answer for me and it is yes. I decided to separate myself once more from the temporal logic and seek for the designs of my Eternal Father. It was one of the most wonderful experiences of my life. In my travels to Israel, I have been targeted with weapons, they have broken into the rooms of our hotels and have left us death threats, among other such events. However, the joy and boldness that we have experienced in these moments resulted in a fullness that only those who are willing to fall asleep to the temporal system and awake to the glory of Jesus can distinguish. In that same land, I could see many men and women, small and great, who are being lost in the business of Satan. They are literally giving their lives to stop the people of the Cross and the chosen ones of God. At this point, I need to ask you some questions: What business are you investing your life in? Are you doing what you want or what your Father wants? Are you running after the sweets of this world or after eternal glory? When a person is moved from slave to son and their identity is restored, the inheritance is activated. We connect with God's plans for the earth. We cease to invest in our own personal kingdom and begin to live only to see His will established in the nations. What used to attract us before no longer seduces us so much. That for which we used to give all our strength, loses its value and we begin to lose ourselves from this temporal world, in order to find ourselves immersed in the business of the Eternal Father.

Where is Little Jesus?

The Bible is full of information about Jesus' ministry from the age of thirty to thirty-three years of age. However, we have little data from His childhood and teenage years. We do not know much about His youth and growth. Many times we tend to observe the finished product in men of God standing on a platform or in the middle of the action, but we are not aware of how their stages of development have been. Everyone goes through processes. Jesus went through thirty years of preparation for only three years of ministry. What a paradox that in the contemporary Church people prepare themselves during three years for thirty years of ministry! We do not like to go through God's dealings, which are meant to train us to be healthy and effective leaders. Every person who is used without being processed, becomes corrupted. Slaves avoid processes, children pay the price of staying in the house.

In Luke chapter 2, a small window opens to see the pre-adolescence of Jesus. This anecdote that the doctor tells in the gospel can give us a little light on the process of this Son of intimacy in His youth. The lad of Nazareth at the age of twelve. What do boys at that age do today? They play football, watch TV, play video games (I think I'm describing a twenty-five-year-old boy!). In most cases, you have to encourage them and insist for them to go to church, as they find it more boring than going to school. What was Jesus like when He was twelve? Let's go to the biblical account. Once a year the feast of Passover was celebrated in Jerusalem. Undoubtedly, it was one of the most important events for the Jewish people, when they remembered the divine liberation from the Egyptian yoke. Special meals, late night dinners, dances, music, and joy were the components of this holiday. Every year children looked forward to the date. I remember when we were little we used to attend an annual party in our small town called "annual fires." They were incredible events with folk dances, music, games. Every year we longed for that moment of encounter with our friends, family, and the whole town. I understand the excitement the children had as the Passover celebration approached. Think of a trip with your family and friends to spend a week celebrating in the most important city of the nation. It happened like that. I imagine the entire caravan excited and happy, singing along the way. Seven wonderful days passed by. It was time to leave the great city and return to Nazareth. Along the way, they shared the anecdotes of the nights before. Suddenly, Joseph asked Mary, *Have you seen little Jesus? Is He with His cousins and friends?* They began to search for Him throughout the caravan. It was so large that they spent an entire day trying to find the young man. After a whole day of searching, they went into despair because Jesus did not appear. Only a mother who has lost her child can understand how the heart beats in those circumstances. Finally, they decided to return to the big city. For three days they looked over all places and found no trace of the child. I can imagine the anguish that Joseph and Mary went through. On the other hand, how would Jesus be after so many days without His parents? Was He desperate, anguished? Mary may have said to Joseph, *He must be crying and looking for me everywhere, how we can be such bad parents?*

At last they found Him. Where was He?

> *"Now so it was that after three days they found Him*
> *in the temple, sitting in the midst of the teachers, both*
> *listening to them and asking them questions. And all*

> *who heard Him were astonished at His understanding*
> *and answers. So when they saw Him, they were amazed;*
> *and His mother said to Him, «Son, why have You done*
> *this to us? Look, Your father and I have sought You*
> *anxiously.» And He said to them, «Why did you seek*
> *Me? Did you not know that I must be about My Father's*
> *business?» But they did not understand the statement*
> *which He spoke to them."*
>
> **Luke 2:46-50, NKJV**

At the age of twelve, Jesus was lost in the Father's business. Attracted by the Scriptures, the temple, and the Kingdom, He had disconnected Himself from time and space. It was not for an hour, not even for one day, but three. Where did He sleep? What did He eat? The Bible does not answer my questions. Apparently, they were not things Jesus was worried about. He did not understand the anguish of His parents, as they did not understand the passion for God in His heart. The chapter ends stating that Jesus grew in wisdom and stature, and in favor with God and men.

God is raising up a generation of men and women who are getting lost in the Father's business. Everybody goes in one direction, the caravan of this world has a fixed course and a clear destination: an assured future, human comforts, material successes, passing vainglories, and temporary pleasures. However, you will not find the sons and daughters of intimacy there. They do not go after the "sweets" of this system, they are strayed into eternal affairs. Do not look for them where common sense says they should be. You will not find them there. They are sons of the wind who are following the breath from the Father's mouth. They are not forging an economic future nor building secure castles for themselves. Something greater has attracted them. It does not matter if they are twelve or sixty years old. They are those who God is preparing for the revolution that is to manifest. The children of intimacy are not understood, just as Jesus' parents did not understand what He was talking about. Some call them fanatics, others call them extreme ones, but there they are submerged in the Word of God. They correspond to every biblical prophecy, cultivating lives of intimacy and worship, preaching the Gospel in time and out of time. They are not going after temporary wages, but claiming an eternal inheritance. Please do not look for them in the crowd because you're going to waste your time. The word "business" refers to activity, action; we can say it means "denying leisure." It has to do with activation. There are many Christians who get bored in Church. The world anesthetizes the children of God for the things that really matter. It entertains them with a deadly leisure. It happens with marriages, teens, and elders. I see a caravan of young people who go after the pleasures of the flesh. They are wasting their best years, those of greater vigor and strength, in matters that are not worth it. At eighteen years old, I found myself living alone in another country, in a seminary, lost in the Father's business. At twenty-one, I founded the MiSion Institute. They told me that I was too young, that the young people of my age had to be engaged in other matters. That the ministry would not give me an economic assurance or a professional future. But something greater had captivated me. I just wanted to honor the Father and see my generation responding to His love. My testimony is clear, while I was seeking for the Kingdom and His righteousness, everything was added to me. I am not saying that everyone has a full-time call in the temple, but I do believe that we all have been called to extend the Kingdom all the time and everywhere. Whether it be through a company, a profession, a trade, a sport, or a ministerial job, we must all live fully for the glory of God for we were created to do that. However, the world draws us like that sweets salesman once captivated me and when we finally react, life has taken us away from the Father and His business. I believe in a remnant who does not kneel down before Baal nor kisses him, as in the time of Elijah.[29] These will overcome the system, denying the leisure of this world and activating themselves in the eternal plans. God is casting these prophets as arrows into every nation and city with a mighty anointing. They have been lost from the caravan, from the world, the flesh, and religion. Just like that man who is described in the Gospels, they have found a treasure in the middle of a field and they sold everything they had to buy that land.[30] It did not cost them much, but everything. They may lose their family or friends, but they are where the Father wants them to be and from that place they will be cast as foundation builders of the latter glory.

God's Co-workers

"For we are co-workers in God's service; you are God's field, God's building."
1 Corinthians 3:9, NIV

God wants to work with His children. We are co-workers. I love when my daughter helps me. Sometimes her contribution may not be so significant but I am glad that we do it together. When they bring the twenty-liter water drums to our house, I push them and she wants to collaborate with me. She does not have the strength to move them for even a millimeter, but she wants to support her dad. She puts her little hands on the drums and pushes with all her might while I put my hands on hers and produce the movement. Religion makes us believe that we are the ones moving the water drums, but it is God who does. Paul taught that it was not about him, not about Apollos, but about God.[31] We simply collaborate. It is the power of

His force what works in us. The Bible teaches us about the work God wants to carry out at this time in the nations. Here are four key events that God, in His Word, made clear that would happen. They are placed chronologically and prophetically in the times we are living. They are water drums and He is moving them. Do you want to help Him? He loves that you put your hands into His affairs.

1. The Spirit Will Be Poured Out on All Flesh

> *"It will come about after this that I will pour out My*
> *Spirit on all mankind; and your sons and daughters*
> *will prophesy, your old men will dream dreams, your*
> *young men will see visions."*
> **Joel 2:28, NASB**

The prophet places this event before the great and dreadful day of the Lord. That is, the second coming of Christ. We are in the fulfillment time of the outpouring of the Spirit on all flesh. We need sons and daughters to collaborate with what the Father wants to do. It will be a time of manifestation of the power of Heaven on earth in a way never seen before. We are on this revival's eve. The only needed thing is children who are willing to wake up to prophecy and reclaim the inheritance of this generation. The Kingdom of God does not consist of words but of power.[32] God has the strength to do so. However, He chose to have it happen through His children. God has shown me that there will be a great manifestation of power in small places. It is not about big structures but about little willing hearts. In every place where there is a beloved son or daughter, the Heavens will be opened, the voice of the Father will be heard, and the Spirit will descend in a visibly way. "Jordan Rivers," deserts, mangers, and prisons are God's favorite places to display His power. Your home, work place, cell group, and weekly worship service will be the settings where Joel's prophecy will be fulfilled. I also believe that there is a very powerful manifestation of God in worship. Worship produces the seat where His glory rests. It is time to worship without ceasing. This genuine cry of His children will be like a magnet to the power of God. The signs will begin to follow those who believe. That is why it is time to worship everywhere, at home, in the temple, in the streets, in squares, and stadiums. As Elijah has experienced, where there are altars, there will be fire and every prophet of God is worth four hundred of Baal's prophets. For every worshiper who awakens in true faith to build public altars, Satan will have to use four hundred of his own, and even then he will not be able to overtake them to stop His worship.

Can God count on you?

2. The Church Will be Glorious, Holy, Without Spot or Wrinkle for Jesus

> *"That He might present her to Himself a glorious church,*
> *not having spot or wrinkle or any such thing, but that*
> *she should be holy and without blemish."*
>
> **Ephesians 5:27**

God is building a glorious Church.[33] He Himself formed leaders to lead the saints to the unity of faith, to the building up of His body and to guide them to the measure of the stature of the perfect Man.[34] We need sons and daughters to collaborate with what the Father is doing. As a pastor, I do not want to build my own church, I want to collaborate with what Jesus is building: *"Unless the Lord builds the house, they labor in vain who build it."*[35] We need people who are lost in the Father's business. God is committed to forming a glorious

Bride. Perhaps the mid-road storms made us believe that the Church is now more corrupt than ever, but God already has a plan and it is already in progress. Will He find children who collaborate with Him in the restoration of the Beloved of Jesus? God is going to take away everything strange from the Church and lead her to virginity. The end result will be to present her pure for Jesus. Heaven is looking for those who are going to pray and work for the purification of the Church. This will be a generation that will exchange criticism, rebellion, and judgment, for love, mercy, and acts of restoration. John the Baptist defined himself as a friend of the Bridegroom.[36] He said: *He who has the bride is the Bridegroom." As His friend, I just want to give my life so that union becomes stronger and deeper. That is our function. As friends of the Bridegroom, we cannot make the Bride fall in love with us. Our greatest purpose is to get the Church to fall in love with Jesus, not with us.* Woe to those who seduce the Beloved of Jesus after themselves! Neither can we criticize or mistreat the Lord's chosen One. The Church is not temples, institutions, or walls, but living stones. Lives that have been chosen by God for a supreme and eternal plan. It is time to wake up for those who weave the garment and perfume the Church for the wedding of the Lamb. The Father wants a Bride for His Son, and the Son wants a Wife for eternity. The Spirit and the Church are eager for this eternal encounter. God is going to awaken leaders and teachers who will lead the Church to an eternal romance. Those who will collaborate with the restoration of the Church are those who are more interested in loving people and guiding them to Him than those who seek only the lights and platforms of religion. Can God count on you?

3. Testimony of the Gospel in All Nations

*"And this gospel of the kingdom will be preached in
all the world as a witness to all the nations, and then
the end will come."*
Matthew 24:14, NKJV

Before the end, there will be an awakening in the Church for loving and preaching Jesus in the nations. We are facing the greatest harvest of souls in history. The countries of the earth are the inheritance of the sons and daughters. Nations are more than territories or political spaces, they are lives. By restoring the identity of His children, God will restore their inheritance. Being locked up within themselves, with a limited and selfish vision, was a mistake in which the people of Israel and the Church fell again and again during centuries. The excuse that if we do not evangelize our neighborhood we cannot go to other nations, is logical, but not biblical. We must testify in our Jerusalem, our Samaria and even to the end of the earth. We need to shine in our neighborhoods, while shining the world. Pastor Bill Johnson says, *The farther away the light shines, the more powerful it is around itself.* We are that lighthouse, the farther our light reaches, the stronger it becomes in our context. I have traveled to many nations and I have seen that the churches which pray, engage themselves, and send ministers to other nations are the ones growing the most and reaching their own cities. Since I began to pray and travel to other continents, our ministry became more powerful in Buenos Aires. The Church of the end times will have a global vision. She will pray, go, give offerings, and send men and women to preach to the nations. I believe this is a great debt that the Western Church has with the whole world. The spiritual move we are living in our American continent must produce fruits that will touch the East. God will fill the eternal Kingdom of people from every race, language, tribe, and nation. He is already doing it. He is only looking for sons and daughters who want to collaborate with His movements.

Can God count on you?

4. The Earth Will Be Filled with the Knowledge of His Glory

"For the earth will be filled with the knowledge of the glory of the Lord, as the waters cover the sea."
Habakkuk 2:14, NKJV

Glory is the visible manifestation of the invisible God. It is the nature and beauty of God. The earth is already full of His glory, but the time comes when everything will be flooded by His revelation just like a tsunami. God is already removing the veils of many and manifesting the delights emanating from Jesus' heart. In the coming times, there will be such a manifestation of the goodness of Jehovah that the people in the nations will be drawn to Him. *"Afterward the sons of Israel will return and seek the Lord their God and David their king; and they will come trembling to the Lord and to His goodness in the last days"* (Hosea 3:5). Another version says, *"They will tremble in awe of the Lord and of His goodness"* (NLT). Can you imagine everything that is about to happen? Our soul will experience an expression of love and divine goodness that produce a tremor in the human body because of the wonder and marvels. A generation of children consumed by His eternal beauty will become those waves of the Spirit that will bring the display of the Father's nature on earth. The glory will be revealed and in God's great eternal script, there will be a day when everyone will see His beauty and splendor. The curtains of Heaven will open and those who have collaborated with God will manifest along with Him. Before the statement we have just read from Habakkuk, the prophet said on behalf of God that we must wait with expectation and work looking forward to that day. That we must write it and declare it:

> *"For the vision is yet for the appointed time; it hastens*
> *toward the goal and it will not fail. Though it tarries,*
> *wait for it; for it will certainly come, it will not delay."*
> **Habakkuk 2:3, NASB**

The Father is at work. He's moving His water drums. It is time for you to put your hands in the plow and do not look back. *Life is too short to spend it on things that will not strengthen your eternity.* Salvation is free, but rewards are earned. The Bible is full of eternal rewards for those who desire to collaborate with the Father. I pray that God will close your eyes to the sweet things of this world. I claim for your spirit to awaken to that which keeps Heaven sleepless and busy in these dramatic times. It's time for you to change directions. You are a son and heir. It does not matter where the caravan goes to. It's time to get lost. I already did. If you want to find me, you know where to search for me.

PRACTICAL GUIDE CHAPTER 9

· *Lost in the Father's Business* ·

Questions to share in groups, cells or leadership teams:

1. What are the "sweets" of this world that are taking God's children out of the Father's business?

2. How can we collaborate with the Father's desire to pour out His Spirit on all flesh? Propose practical and creative ideas.

3. How can we collaborate with the Father's desire to restore His Church as a glorious Bride, spotless and wrinkleless? Propose practical and creative ideas.

4. How can we collaborate with the Father's desire that the Gospel be preached to the ends of the earth? Propose practical and creative ideas.

5. How can we collaborate with the Father's desire to manifest His glory and beauty in this generation? Propose practical and creative ideas.

Personal application exercise:

Write a plan to connect your current activities (work, studies, ministry, family) with God's plans for this hour on earth. How can you align your life and agenda with the desires of God's heart for this generation?

CHAPTER 10

· Awake to the Glory of the Father ·

A life of intimacy, devotion, adoration, and passionate communion with God is not another biblical ministry but the fuel for all ministries–apostolic, prophetic, pastoral, evangelistic, and teaching–to be effective.

When the heart is dazzled by the eternal realm, it falls asleep to the temporal things.

Before God uses your hands, the devil will always want to dirty them up.

When we let the flesh corrupt our intimacy, our heart becomes a stone.

CHAPTER 10

· Awake to the Glory of the Father ·

Iwould like to begin this chapter with two biblical scenes. One of them takes place in the Sea of Galilee. Jesus gave a speech and then told His friends to get across to the other side. It happens to the disciples as it happens with many of us in the middle of the road: storms, tempests, doubts, and anxieties. It often seems that the rough weather of life has more power than the words of Jesus. That's what happened to them. I would like you to observe the picture for a moment: the disciples are awake and Jesus is sleeping. They are in despair and the Master is resting. Why does Jesus fall asleep over the very circumstances that concern us? My conclusion is this: what makes men worry, makes Jesus sleepy. Many of Jesus' disciples are awake to matters that the Lord does not care about. He is not there. What keeps man awake is not the same thing that keeps Jesus awake. Today faith is preached to buy a car, a house, or to have a raise. Hebrews 11, the most powerful expression of what faith is throughout the Bible, teaches us that faith is to conquer kingdoms, perform acts of righteousness, obtain promises, shut the mouths of lions, quench the power of fire, escape the edge of the sword, from weakness become strong, become mighty in war, put foreign armies to flight. We are awake to the system of this world and asleep to Jesus.

Here's the second scene. It is also about yawning and sleeping. Now we move to Gethsemane. Jesus is awake, He is going through His most critical moment on earth. His will is to die there. In the midst of His anguish He asks His disciples to remain awake praying. What happens? They fall asleep. Not once, but three times. On these occasions, Jesus asks them to wake up to what was happening to Him and accompany Him in His burdens. They do not respond. They fall asleep to that which bears the heart of Jesus. In the first scene, they stay awake and Jesus is asleep. Now, Jesus is awake and they surrender to sleep. *That which is important to Jesus, makes men sleep.* What does keep awake the heart of the Lord today? Are His contemporary disciples responding to it? The Bible tells us that God will not repose nor give rest to His eyes until He sees some events happening on earth. Jesus intercedes before the Father, the Spirit leads us to the truth. The Trinity is awake and operating in the nations. What about the sons? Are they awake to the Father or to the system? Are they engaged in what God wants to do in nations or are they preoccupied with their little temporal world? The sons and daughters are lost in the Father's business. It is wonderful to see how a spirit of revelation and wisdom unleashes the knowledge of Christ and the understanding of the times within those who are willing to fall asleep to the system and wake up to Jesus. We need a revival, an awakening. Temporary storms make Jesus sleep, so we must rest, too. The affairs of the eternal Kingdom that keep Jesus awake must wake up us as well. God keeps Himself awake for Israel according to Isaiah 62. He is also busy in bringing the Church into intimacy, restoring her identity as children and as the Bride of the Lamb. He is working in order to ignite His people to be light in the darkest time. He wants to bring them out of comfort and into a true life of faith. He is awakening His chosen ones to the revelation of Jesus, the Bridegroom, the Judge, and the King, that was clearly prophesied for the last times. He is recruiting men and women for the plan of restoration of all things, of all families, and of all nations. Now, what is keeping you awake?

Awakening to the Glory of Jesus

In order to see the glory of God, we must stay awake. We become what we look at. The focus of our life determines our purpose. In this season, Jesus longs to show you facets of His person, beauty, and character that will bring about a permanent transformation in your life. For this, you must identify everything that wants to numb you. Satan's goal is to distract you so that your eyes will not look to the right place. In several biblical passages, we can identify the devil's plan to numb the Church of the end times. He will try to make her sleep in the pleasures and comforts of the world. The parable of the ten virgins[37] clearly describes how this spiritual dream will come upon the whole world, upon the wise and the foolish. In this context, Jesus calls His people to watch over ten times. To watch, means to be awake while others sleep. The very religious system makes the disciples fall asleep to the eternal purpose. The children of religion are on the alert for circumstances that make Jesus sleep. The Christian life becomes overwhelming and boring. The yoke of Jesus is easy and His burden is light.[38] However, the system puts weights on our shoulders that end up pushing us down. With a historical and theoretical gospel, it's burying many of God's children, making them live as slaves and orphans. In that context, I can see Jesus preparing for you a transforming and liberating encounter, as He did with Nicodemus. In the formation process of the disciples there was an event that marked a turning point in their lives. Walking with the Master of Nazareth was eclipsed by a glorious manifestation of the Christ of Glory, and that affected the apostles' life forever. I'm talking about the Transfiguration. An instant in which the life of the beloved disciples of the Lord was wrapped into a revelation of the power, beauty, and glory of Jesus, and it made them awake to eternal purposes. In the Epistles and Gospels, we will see how this event became the fuel and propellant of their ministries. In order to have a meeting of such a dimension with the glory of Jesus, we must take into account some principles.

The Mount of Intimacy

"Now it came to pass, about eight days after these sayings, that He took Peter, John, and James and went up on the mountain to pray."
Luke 9:28, NKJV

When God wants to reveal some new aspects of His glory, He takes you to the mount of intimacy. Note that He did not take all His disciples, but only those who longed to be closer to Him. Just as a hunger for intimacy and to be closer to Jesus was awakened in Nicodemus, you should channel the desire that led you to have this book in your hands in order to approach the Holy Mount like never before. God is taking you to a place where He wants to reveal Himself to you in a different way. The disciples were accustomed to seeing Jesus of Nazareth, but they were about to discover the Christ of Glory. They were about to be changed from the knowledge of a great historical Man into a Heavenly and eternal One. They believed that they walked with a mighty Man who performed many miracles, but God was introducing them into the reality that the One they followed was far more beautiful, glorious, and eternal than any other. When God calls you to the mount of intimacy, it's because He wants to reveal to you some divine and eternal aspects impossible to be created by religion. Hebrews 8:5 details that it was on the mountain that Moses received the Heavenly model to build the tabernacle. Up there, God gave him the plans with details, measurements, and colors of what he had to build on the earth. The children of intimacy, who express the designs of the Father in the generations, receive the Heavenly models in the mount of intimacy. It's there, where His Divinity permeates your face and others begin to see Christ in you—the hope of glory. That's the place of prophetic direction and Divine instruction. *A life of intimacy, devotion, adoration, and passionate communion with God is not another biblical ministry but the fuel for all ministries—apostolic, prophetic, pastoral, evangelistic, and teaching—to be effective.* When God calls His disciples to intimacy, He wants to empower them to do something in the public. Once we respond to this supreme calling, we need to develop a lifestyle to remain there.

The Process of Intimacy

"As He prayed, the appearance of His face was altered,
and His robe became white and glistening."
Luke 9:29, NKJV

As prayer flows, something glorious begins to manifest itself. Intimacy is not an event, but a process. It has more to do with remaining than going. Intimacy focuses on His face. Up to this point, the disciples were delighted by the hands of Jesus, His miracles and power. However, the glory that transforms lives is found in His face.[39] We all, with unveiled faces, beholding as in a mirror the glory of the Lord, are being transformed into the same image of Jesus.[40] This verb speaks of a present continuous, it's not about an event, but a process of remaining with our eyes fixed on Him. This attitude of passion and devotion introduces us to the manifestation of His glory. Suddenly, in the midst of prayer and worship, Jesus begins to transfigure Himself and His intimate ones begin to see aspects of His person that were unknown. His appearance is changed, His robe is stained with indescribable bright colors, and the Divinity of their Leader captivates them. They are those who climb the mount of intimacy and remain in that attitude of seeking His face, those who discover facets of Christ that religion cannot teach. While the system creates boring Christians, who believe they already know everything about God, the sons and daughters of intimacy are entering into the reality that the infinite glory of the preexisting Being cannot be limited by human wisdom. In other words, eternity will not be enough for us to reach and finish discovering all the attributes that emanate from the inexhaustible Source of wonders. This revelation of Jesus, marvels and affects the inner part of men, captivating them irreversibly and consuming their fleshly passions and desires. David explained it this way:

> *"Wonderful are Your works, and my soul knows*
> *it very well."*
>
> **Palms 139:14b, NASB**

When the heart is dazzled by the eternal realm, it falls asleep to the temporal things. Christ revealed produces a higher pleasure in the human interior, which no system of this world can even be compared to. The problem is that many know the historical Jesus, but have not climbed the mount of intimacy to meet the glory of God. Moses had experienced mighty miracles, had seen the sea parting in two, he had seen bread falling down from the sky, a pillar of fire suspended in the air, plagues in Egypt, and many other things. However, at one point in his life, he realized that it was not enough to satisfy the inner hunger he had to be marveled and contented with something. And that's when he exclaimed: *"I pray You, show me Your glory!"*[41] It was on the mountain where he received this revelation of divine features of the face and character of God that affected him forever. He never wanted anything else. When God offered Him a tremendous ministerial future, granting Him to be the greatest leader of the hour, freeing His people from bondage, He rather preferred His glory. *"If Your Presence does not go with us, do not bring us up from here."*[42] The children of intimacy rather prefer the Presence of God than ministerial success. They are not willing to have the recognition of men, if they cannot enjoy the eternal glory within them.

This experience so affected His disciples that it became the foundation of their ministries. John introduces his gospel with these words about the experience of transfiguration:

> *"And the Word became flesh and dwelt among us, and*
> *we beheld His glory, the glory as of the only begotten of*
> *the Father, full of grace and truth."*
> **John 1:14, NKJV**

The intimate disciple underlies everything he is going to write about Jesus claiming that he had contemplated His Divinity. Studying the beauty of Jesus, contemplating His face, and more deeply understanding His divine attributes, are the fuel of the eternal Kingdom's messengers in the temporal world. The revelation of Jesus acquired in intimacy is the greatest source of power and authority in the sons and daughters of God. As founder and director of a center for Bible and ministerial studies, I assure you that this dimension of which I am speaking about cannot be given to you by a seminar. There, you will be able to acquire tools that will take you to the Holy Mount. In those settings, God will awaken a deep desire within you to respond to His heart. This is a great and important addition, but it cannot replace the most important thing: your life of devotion, prayer, adoration, and intimacy with God on the mount. That place of exposure to the beauty of Jesus' face is the propelling fire that will launch your life to the purposes of God on earth in a powerful and effective way.

Let's look at Peter talking about this experience in his letter:

> *"For we did not follow cunningly devised fables when we made known to you **the power and coming of our Lord Jesus Christ**, but were eyewitnesses of His majesty. For He received from God the Father honor and glory when such a voice came to Him from the Excellent Glory: «This is My beloved Son, in whom I am well pleased.» And we heard this voice which came from heaven **when we were with Him on the holy mountain.**"*
>
> **2 Peter 1:16-18, NKJV**
> Emphasis added by the author

Peter references the experience on the Mount of Transfiguration as the foundation of his message and ministry. In other words, he is saying all that we preach, announce, and believe are not invented stories, for we have seen His glory on the mount with our own eyes. There are two distinct characteristics of those who live in this dimension of the revelation of Jesus: *They reveal the power of the*

Kingdom in this generation, and they announce the return of Christ. These are two pillars for the children of intimacy who are awakened to the glory of the Father. Before this experience, the disciples knew Jesus of Nazareth, but suddenly they began to discover the face and appearance of the Christ of Glory, who sits at the right hand of the Father, clothed with majesty, and who is coming to reign over all nations. When the children of God do not spend time on the mount of intimacy, they preach and live a historical Jesus. Instead, those who live in the Father's lap have access to the revelation, not only of what He did, but also what He is doing today, and what is about to happen.

In this process of intimacy, Peter, James, and John, had access to an important detail: Moses and Elijah were speaking with Jesus in His glory.

> *"And behold, two men were talking with Him; and*
> *they were Moses and Elijah, who, appearing in glory,*
> *were speaking of His departure which He was about to*
> *accomplish at Jerusalem."*
>
> **Luke 9:30-31, NASB**

Moses represents the Law, and Elijah represents the prophets. They were both talking about what it was about to happen. Suddenly, in this glorious experience of intimacy, everything is connected. The Law and the prophets lead to Jesus. Everything leads to His glory. I understand that the disciples receive a deep understanding of the purpose for the laws of the people of Israel and the prophets. The religious were experts in the Commandments and words these envoys of God had declared for generations, but they could not link them to what was happening in those days or to what was about to happen. One experience with the glory of Jesus gives meaning to the whole Word. Suddenly, those who remain on the mountain begin to understand how everything speaks of Christ and His return. The mount of intimacy is a place of revelation of the Scriptures and of prophetic instruction about the next steps that Jesus will give. In this place, all the prior knowledge we have about God is redeemed, and then we can say as the righteous Job: *"I have heard of You by the hearing of the ear, but now my eye sees You."*[43]

Although all this is wonderful, the best thing has not yet happened on the mountain. Those who remain in the heights of intimacy go from glory to glory and they are transformed to be more like Him.

Staying Awake

We can perceive when God awakens our inner self to His glory. It is not an experience that we live with the external senses, but rather something unlocks in the depths of our being, and we begin to feel attracted by the attributes of Jesus and consumed by His desires. He unleashes an indescribable love, a fervent yearning to be with Him and collaborate with His will. We identify those moments in a powerful time of worship in which we recognize the Presence of God behind the music, or we hear a prophetic and anointed ministry and identify the voice of the Spirit behind the words. Sometimes, that awakening occurs through phrases expressed in a book when we recognize that the writer is the pen, but the source of those words is God Himself. The means may be a worship conference, an experience of power with God in the streets, a talk with a friend of the Kingdom, or an instant of Divine visitation when we are drawn to His love. However, if we do not continue doing these things, these isolated events fade away. The secret is to remain there, because the weeks of routine and temptations seem to be much longer than the weekends of glory. Perhaps the fuel we receive at that challenging camp or at the revival congress, is quickly consumed in the mileage of the daily walk. The dream returns to what is important and we lose ourselves in the caravan of this world. Only a lifestyle of devotion and passion for the heart of God, can keep us on the mount and expose us to His transforming glory.

Let's see the end of the experience of these three intimate ones on the mountain. They were living a turning point moment in their lives. However, even when they were watching this glorious revelation, the sleep wanted to conquer them.

> *"Now Peter and his companions had been overcome with sleep;* ***but when they were fully awake, they saw His glory*** *and the two men standing with Him."*
>
> **Luke 9:32**
> Emphasis added by the author

They were in the midst of a supreme and divine moment, but the dream increased within them. In the key situations of your life, Satan will try to make you sleep to what is worthy. You must fight. You cannot give up. *Before God uses your hands, the devil will always want to dirty them up.* A great victory is preceded by a terrible struggle. These three disciples of Jesus were very sleepy. You may ask: How can they fall asleep at such a glorious manifestation? In response, I want to ask you: How can you be worried and anxious for temporal circumstances, when Christ is taking your life to wonderful dimensions and yearning to reveal His glory to you? How can we be distracted when the King of Glory is ready to return, to ordain the earth, and to rule all nations? Why do we exchange indescribable eternal plans for bowls of beans of temporal endeavors? All the Law and the prophets spoke about this time. One hundred and fifty chapters in the Bible describe the end times and the events God will unleash in our age (and believe me, they are wonderfully impressive). In the two hundred and sixty chapters of the New Testament, we find three hundred and eighteen references to the glorious return of Christ to earth. There is something that is about to unfold, we are about to see dimensions of His majesty as we never have before. We must fight spiritual laziness, diabolic anesthesia, and temporary blurring, so that we do not miss what God wants to reveal to us. Despite the sleep, they stayed awake. Then they saw the glory of Jesus. What is the secret? Despite the struggling against all strategies to numb your purpose, keep awake to Jesus. Do not take your eyes off Him, persevere in prayer and worship. You have to begin enjoying and delighting in His love. You must cross the line of passivity, fight for what will really transcend. You can determine within yourself not to give place to spiritual sleep, you can pray not to fall into temptation. I would like to tell you as Paul told the Ephesians: *"Awake, you who sleep, arise from the dead, and Christ will give you light."*[44] This light will bring understanding, revelation, and divine activation within you. The eyes of your spiritual understanding will be enlightened. What you see will attract you much more than the delights of this century. Those who persevere in the mount of intimacy, contemplate the beauty of Jesus and become messengers of His power, returning to the nations. *When we let the flesh corrupt our intimacy, our heart becomes a stone.* We lose sensitivity to what He wants to show us. Now, identify everything that wants to get you out of that place. You must sleep to lots of circumstances and problems Jesus is not concerned about. If He is in the boat of your life, everything will be fine, but Jesus is awake because of the greater matters of the Kingdom. He wants you to stay awake with Him. You have to develop the lifestyle of remaining in His love. As you make intimacy your home, you will begin to receive the revelation of His glory, and it will captivate all your being. Then whatever captivates the Heavens, will make you fall in love even more.

For the disciples, it was a day on the Mount of Transfiguration; for Moses, it was, forty days at Sinai; for Nicodemus, it was a night with Jesus. All these places have something in common: God was awakening key people in order to transform them into spiritual parents for generations. I have written most of the chapters of this book in such a way that you have a revelation of the love of the Father and the glory of Jesus who redefines you as son or daughter of intimacy. I am convinced that, as you were reading these pages, your identity as son or daughter has been restored and that all orphanhood and slavery have been consumed. I believe that as you cultivate your life of intimacy with the Father, you will have to come down from the mount and impart to others the love you have received. In the next chapter, I want to talk to you about this. Along the way of living as a child of intimacy, you will become a father or mother for many orphans, a reference of the love and character of the Father for others. The Mount of Transfiguration was not the final destination, but a process in which God was forming those followers into the early church apostles. A face-to-face encounter with the Father's love and the glory of Jesus is the beginning of your activated purpose on earth. Are you ready for the next step? You will become a spiritual father or mother for many orphans in this generation.

PRACTICAL GUIDE CHAPTER 10
· *Awake to the Glory of the Father* ·

Questions to share in groups, cells or leadership teams:

1. What are the temporary storms of this system that try to make the children of God "sleep" so that they cannot see the glory of the Father?

2. What attitudes lead us to rise to a new level of intimacy with God?

3. How important is it to "abide" in a lifestyle of intimate devotion with God, to see His glory and bear fruit that glorifies the Father? How can we achieve it?

4. What circumstances keep Jesus awake in this generation?

Personal application exercise:

Under what circumstances is God asking you to fall asleep? What is shaking your boat at this time? Are you awake to that which keeps Jesus awake? How much do you long to see the glory of the Father and what are you willing to do to see it? Write your answers below.

____

____

____

____

CHAPTER 11

· Parents of Generations ·

*This generation does not need
superheroes or evangelical stars, but
parents who love and see them as
God does.*

*A small group of children impacted
by their intimacy with Jesus is much
more powerful than the crowds
impressed by His miracles.*

*God is not an idol to be worshiped on
Sundays. He is a Father with whom
we walk daily. And those who live
in intimate union with God are the
ones who manifest Him.*

*Many people listened to the Master's
sermons, but only those who walked
with Him in intimacy
were transformed.*

CHAPTER 11

· *Parents of Generations* ·

A few years ago, I saw a young man entering MiSion Institute. He came to offer piano lessons, but God had brought him for something much greater. As soon as I saw him, I knew he had a glorious purpose and a prophetic destiny in his life. I perceived an essence so pure within him, as I have not seen in anyone else before. However, his face and some of his attitudes seemed disconnected from the definition of Heaven over his life. Some months passed, but we still had almost no relationship. I noticed that he was a man of intimacy with God and that he loved Jesus. Although he believed that no one was watching him, I followed his movements carefully and prayed for God to show me what was behind the impression I was receiving of him. At times he seemed distracted and lonely, sometimes even angry. I did not know why, but God was connecting him with me. I invited him on some ministerial trips to play the keyboard and to accompany me in the ministry. I was trying to get close, like someone looking for treasure in the middle of an ocean. We started to have a good time, but we did not manage to deepen the relationship. However, there was a day that marked a breaking point. We were in a youth camp, and the time came when God brought me the clarity of what He was up to with all this. I received a very strong word for his life.

I approached him, embraced him, and released what God was saying to me: *Two times Satan has called you an orphan, but Heaven calls you a son. From this day on, I will live to be a spiritual father to you. God takes away all orphanhood off from you, and He will use you to bring paternity to the nations. You are the father of orphans, the father of this generation.* For the next few minutes he cried and something was released inside of him. I did not fully understand what was happening. My quick interpretation was that maybe he would have a bad relationship with his father and probably with his pastor, that's why he was twice called orphan by the enemy. However, upon hearing his testimony later, my heart broke. When he was little, he was eight years old, he had lost his biological father because of a terminal illness. The relationship with him had not been good, and his memories were dark. After this tragic event, his mother rebuilt her life and married a man of God. He had become an exemplary father for him, accompanying him at all times and guiding him on the ways of the Kingdom. Three months before I met him, his second father had died of a very aggressive form cancer. He arrived at MiSion Institute with his soul shattered and his identity confused. The heart of this young man was invaded by orphanhood and sought after acceptance at any price. I then understood why, many times, I used to see him so lost, but now God had taken him to that place of intimacy to redefine him according to Heaven. When he was telling me this, I was amazed at the accuracy of God's words. Listening to the details of what had happened in his family, even with his ancestors, I could see how Satan had always try to abort the purpose of this key man for the Kingdom of God. I literally became a spiritual father to him. We began to walk together for the last few years and witness how God was transforming the life and identity of this young man, not only into a child loved by God, but also into a father of this generation. His name is Agustin, and we have traveled together for years throughout the nations and have seen the beauty of the Beloved One invading cities and hearts. He has an extraordinary talent in music and an impacting heart of a worshiper and prophet. His essence was there from the first day I saw him. God removed the dust that darkened His purpose, and He produced a restoration of supernatural love in him. Many children of intimacy are trying to be aborted and nullified by Satan because they are the parents of a needy generation—a generation longing for someone to see them as Jesus does and to hug them as the Father wants to embrace them.

Jesus the Beloved Son and the Eternal Father

Jesus was never a natural father. However, in His walk as a Beloved Son, He became the father of a generation of orphans. Throughout His life we can find Him singing with His disciples, having John lying on His chest, or cooking a fish for Peter on the beach after he had denied Him. When He is about to leave the earth, He affirms His identity as father and His eternal commitment:

"I will not leave you orphans; I will come to you."
John 14:18

Jesus came to reveal the heart of God by becoming a father to His generation. More than a hero, He wanted to be a dad; more than a master, He wanted to be a friend. In developing His identity as Son, the nature of His Abba was manifested through Him. God's purpose in restoring our essence as His children, is to shape parents for many soul and spirit orphans. These parents will be the ones that God will use to transform children of religion into children of intimacy. In my personal journey, living as a child of God and allowing this identity to develop within me, a spiritual fatherhood began to flow towards many who needed the revelation of the nature of God. *This generation does not need super-heroes or evangelical stars, but parents who love and see them as God does.* Someone once said: from a distance, you can impress; but, if you are near, you can impact. Impressions are transitory, but the impact is eternal. God chose us to leave a transcendental mark in the hearts of spiritual children. *A small group of children impacted by their intimacy with Jesus is much more powerful than the crowds impressed by His miracles.* As we saw in previous chapters, orphanhood has to do with lack of protection, lack of value, and lack of acceptance. Jesus is manifesting Himself as the One who will be with them at all times, even after the Cross. Not only does He want to be a leader who preaches every week in their meetings, He wants to be a dad who walks with them and who will remain committed to them forever. He signs an agreement of protection, value, and acceptance. This is the standard of leadership that, as men and women of God, we must pursue. Just like the disciples of Galilee, every person in our churches and cities needs parents. They need lives who reflect the love and the divine nature in everything. We do not need love to criticize, judge, or describe what is wrong with someone, but we do need love to forgive, honor, and wash their feet even if he is the one who will betray us. We do not necessarily have to be a son or daughter to preach a good sermon, but we do in order to show the essence of God everywhere we go. There can be no family without a father. This is the model of the Heavenly denomination, and so it must be on earth. So, if you are already walking in your identity as a beloved son, it is time to ask yourself: Who are the orphans around you who need to see the Father through your life? What do you yearn for: a superhero of religion or a father of a generation in need of love and identity?

Jesus was never a biological father, however, when Isaiah prophesied about that child to be born, he said:

> *"For a child will be born to us, a son will be given to us;*
> *and the government will rest on His shoulders; and His*
> *name will be called Wonderful Counselor, Mighty God,*
> ***Eternal Father****, Prince of Peace."*

Isaiah 9:6, NASB
Emphasis added by the author

The eternal identity of Jesus is that of a father. This makes you His child forever and ever. Spiritual fatherhood goes far beyond being a natural father or not. It is the response of someone who has left his orphaned position and wants to love others the way he was loved. It is a commitment to those whom God has given us to care for. The Gospels do not describe Jesus' prayers, although they state clear that He was constantly speaking with His Father. In John 17, we find one of the few times where this dialogue with God is recorded. It was the night before the Cross. His final words are captured by the intimate disciple. The topic of His prayer is a sort of accountability to the Father for what He has done on earth. He has finished His work and He has glorified Him. We all have an assigned work, something to build on earth, and in our last sighs we will have to give an account for our earthly accomplishments.[45] However, in His final declaration, the Son of God does not speak about the miracles He has done, nor about the multitudes He has attained, but of "those whom the Father had given Him." He focused on twelve. He cared for them, protected them, and taught them all things. His work did not end on earth for He said He would continue to make known the Father as His Heavenly ministry.[46] Today, Jesus remains committed to revealing the Father to us. He prayed for them all to be one and to love each other. Can you notice the fatherhood within this sentence? The ministry has nothing to do with occupying positions, but with loving people. Slaves focus on tasks, children focus on lives. To do different tasks we do not need a longterm commitment, but in order to disciple people we do. Jude walked for years with Jesus, but when Jesus introduced the covenant, he fled from the table. There are many who flee from commitment. They are orphans, they do not accept paternity. Being a son or daughter implies commitment, just like being a father. It is much more than giving a beautiful teaching or singing an anointed song. It has to do with a covenant. When I travel to the nations, I meditate on this: Performing an act of service (like preaching a sermon, or washing everyone's feet) can take me two or three hours, but committing myself to being a spiritual father and helping those people reach their purposes in God, implies a life committed to disciple them. I have discovered that it is easier to be a servant (who performs a task) rather than a parent (who commits himself to a person). In the way of exercising your spiritual fatherhood over whom God has given you, you will perform miracles, you will preach to multitudes, you will multiply bread and fishes, you will record CDs, you will write books, and who knows how much more. But, you must never forget that being like Jesus is to be a loving father who walks among and with people—loving, forgiving, and showing others what Heaven says about them.

He Who Sees the Son, Sees the Father

*"«If you had known Me, you would have known My
Father also; from now on you know Him, and have seen
Him.» Philip said to Him, «Lord, show us the Father, and
it is enough for us.» Jesus said to him, «Have I been so
long with you, and yet you have not come to know Me,
Philip? He who has seen Me has seen the Father; how can
you say, Show us the Father»".*

John 14:7-9, NASB

Jesus is the tangible manifestation of the invisible God. He reveals the qualities of the Father in every action. There are many "Philips" today shouting: *Show me the Father and that is enough for me.* We need a generation of sons and daughters who reveal Him. Those who dwell in the lap of God, can say as Jesus said: *He who sees the son, sees the Father.* I love it when people say that my daughter looks like me. It fills me with joy and pleasure. God loves when someone tells us that he sees His nature in us. Do the people around you see the Father throughout your life? Can you say like Jesus: I have been with you for so long, and you still do not know what God is like? We need people who would love as Jesus loves, and who would forgive as He forgives. I believe that the most important purpose for which you were born is that others can see Christ in you, the Hope of Glory.[47]

At the end of the last conference Intimacy with the Beloved, someone told me: *You have grown so much. Fifteen nations represented at the conference, hundreds and thousands of people attending it. This is a revival.* But, when a proudly loaded mosquito wanted to bite me, God reminded me that religion measures achievement by numbers and mathematical growth. However, in the Kingdom, success has to do with how many people can see the Father in your life. If anything makes me happy, it is my wife—who knows all my faults and virtues—telling me that she sees Jesus in me every day. That is the measure of success. A minister does not grow because of his increasing fame. True growth in one's life has to do with how much your love for God and for your neighbor has increased. If we are loving more than yesterday, we can say we are moving forward. Many times our ministerial rise and an increase in our love for God are not proportional. We must live so that people see the Father when they look at us. For this to happen, we need to enter into delight with Him and awaken to His glory. *God is not an idol to be worshiped on Sundays. He is a Father with whom we walk daily. And those who live in intimate union with God are the ones who manifest Him.*

"No one has seen God at any time. The only begotten Son, who is in the bosom of the Father, He has declared Him."

John. 1:18, NKJV

The New International Version says that the Son, who is in "*closest relationship with the Father*," has made Him known to us. The "bosom" of the Father refers to His lap. He desires to have us in His lap, to embrace us and take delight in us. This bond of extreme love, leads us to the purpose of manifesting Him to those who want to see Him. When Moses descended from the mount of intimacy, his face was shining with the glory of the Father. When the disciples came down from the Mount of Transfiguration, they began to manifest Jesus. There are many things that can be manufactured in the ministry, but the nature of the Father is not one of them. You can decorate the church, and buy lights, and get the latest sound equipment. You can dress up as an evangelical and speak as such. You will learn to memorize the most anointed preaching you have heard and you can also ask the worship ministry to play the most fashionable song in a sublime way. However, when people see the Father as they look at you, it is something that only comes as a consequence of living a life of intimacy, a life recognizing that before anything else, you are a beloved son, in whom the Father feels pleased. By spending time exposed to His glory, you will be transformed as by the Spirit of the Lord in His very image. And people will see it.

Parents of Orphans

It's amazing how kids are always trying to imitate their parents. My daughter watches me talking on my cell phone and takes her play cell phone and does the same. She has her own plastic versions of a computer, tablet, car, and motorcycle. Her essence is to see what her father does and then imitate him. When did we lose that purity and innocence? Now I do understand why God calls us to be like children in order to receive revelation.[48] Paul said, *"Be imitators of me, just as I also am of Christ."*[49] There are many examples of people in the Bible who led with spiritual fatherhood eradicating all orphanhood from their disciples. Paul himself calls Timothy his beloved son.[50] He told the Corinthians that he was their father:

> *"For if you were to have countless tutors in Christ, yet*
> *you would not have many fathers, for in Christ Jesus I*
> *became your father through the gospel."*
>
> **1 Corinthians 4:15, NASB**

John, the beloved disciple, wrote:

> *"I have no greater joy than this, to hear of my children*
> *walking in the truth."*
>
> **3 John 1:4, NASB**

This intimate man of God is saying that there is something superior to all the glorious experiences and revelations, and this is to see his spiritual children walk in the paths of God. It is expressed by someone who had the joy of walking close to Jesus, seeing Him perform tremendous miracles, receiving unpublished revelations from Heaven; he was in the Pentecost worship and in the early revival years of the early Church. However, he describes a greater joy found in a paternity-discipleship. Surely there is no greater pleasure than having spiritual children and seeing them grow in the wisdom and purpose of God. The Father wants to give you this gift. By the grace of God, I have had the opportunity to share the Word of God in many nations, for hundreds and thousands of people, and this is a wonderful thing. I have witnessed glorious services, countless times, I have seen miracles and people being transformed hundreds of times. However, I recognize this principle, there is no greater joy than having spiritual children and seeing them grow in truth and wholeness. I have discipled people since I was a teenager, and all I have learned about the Kingdom and the ministry has been through getting involved with others and, learning little by little to be a spiritual father. Just as my daughter has taught me to be a father, the discipleship of paternal love is the greatest seminary a child of God can complete.

There is a man in the Bible who was a spiritual father of orphans. He took a lot of indebted, rejected, and marginalized people and transformed them into an army of revival men who established God's rule over a nation. I think we do not realize the potential we have to reach the next generations by leading through spiritual fatherhood. God anointed David with the promise of a kingdom. In the way of his preparation, He took him into the wilderness, fleeing from Saul and his squadrons. God processed his character, revealed Himself before him in intimacy, and prepared him to finally take hold of the promise. For this, He gives David the leadership of four hundred men in the Adullam cave. Samuel describes them as afflicted, in debt, and in bitterness of spirit. In other words: orphans full of loneliness and rejection. We do not know what happened in that cave. What we do know is that the biblical account shows us that these men became powerful warriors, worshipers of God, loyal to David, and that God used them to put the *"man after His own heart"* on the throne of Israel. God assigned Jesus a group of rough and limited workers and He assigned David a band of marginalized men. The common denominator: orphans in need of a father. We cannot send our disciples to build the Church or to form an army if we do not bring the orphanhood out of their hearts first. We want to transform nations and cities, but we are counting on a group of people like the ones Jesus or David had. What then is needed to reach such promises? Spiritual fathers, leading them full of love and appreciation for them, eradicating all orphanhood and showing a model to be imitated. They need to be people who want to mess with those that no one embraces. Leaders who are willing to make a commitment to walk close to them and guide them to their glorious destiny. These should be sons and daughters who show the Father. People used with power by God, but also who never forget where they came from and where they must return, to the Father's lap. How could David not be a father to those anguished men in the cave of Adullam, if in his intimacy with God he did see this characteristic in Him?

> *"A father of the fatherless... is God in His*
> *holy habitation."*
>
> **Psalm 68:5**

From Heroes to Parents

*"«And I will be a father to you, and you shall be sons
and daughters to Me,» says the Lord Almighty."*
2 Corinthians 6:18, NASB

The Jews were expecting a hero, but God sent a father—someone close who shared every moment with them. Jesus was someone who affirmed the identity of His people above their areas of competence. Among His intimates there were fishermen, tax collectors, and revolutionaries, but the Father gave them to Him as children. For many, Jesus was a hero, but for those who revolutionized the earth and established the Lord's glorious Church, He was a Father. *Many people listened to the Master's sermons, but only those who walked with Him in intimacy were transformed.* Religion produces heroes, Heaven produces parents. Religion establishes many thrones, but in the Kingdom there is only one throne and it is Jesus' throne. In the Kingdom, there are no idols, only men and women who reflect the heart of the Father. We need a generation of parents who collaborate with God to eradicate all orphans of this generation. People who are not so focused on the glamor of crowds and recognition, but on those from the world the Father gave us, who are His and whom we have to take care of. Today's Church does not need great sermons and books; she needs a greater love manifested through those who are able to leave their own thrones in order to walk with the orphans of heart.

When God removes from your heart the spirit of orphanhood and reveals the facets of His glory to you, He not only heals your soul and affirms your spirit, but He changes you into a father or mother for this generation. You can then be entrusted with His greatest treasure: the lives that will be transformed into spiritual revolutionaries on earth.

God wants to give you gifts and power so that the darkness recedes. He wants to give you ministry and functions to equip the saints. He wants to make His glory shine on you, but the only foundation for this to happen is to be whole in what He thinks of you: *You are my beloved son and I like you.* You must ask yourself: Do you want to be a hero for this generation or a father/mother reflecting His love?

PRACTICAL GUIDE CHAPTER 11

· *Parents of Generations* ·

Questions to share in groups, cells or leadership teams:

1. What has your relationship with your parents been like and how has that affected your relationship with the eternal Father?

2. Who are the people God has called you to disciple as spiritual children?

3. What are the characteristics of a "spiritual father/mother" who disciple others as Jesus, Paul or John did?

4. How do we eradicate orphanhood from the hearts of God's children?

Personal application exercise:

Write three names of people (there may be more) that you commit to disciple with a fatherhood/motherhood leadership. Write down practical actions that you will do for them to reveal the Father's love to them.

Name: ____

Action: ____

____

____

____

CHAPTER 12

· The Revolution of the Children of God ·

*The sons and daughters who live the
nature of the Father and who cry
Abba, they are the object of desire of
God's heart.*

*Intimacy with God is to enjoy Him
and be enjoyed by the Father.*

*God continues to use grace baskets
to protect those children who will
become liberators.*

*Intimacy brings law to life, though
law always wants to kill intimacy.*

CHAPTER 12

· The Revolution of the Children of God ·

I was at a conference in Rio de Janeiro a few years ago where I met some pastors from Japan. In 2011, an earthquake had devastated that nation. The pastor told me how dramatic it was to have lived through that historic and gigantic tremor right from the front row. Anti-seismic buildings looked like paper in the face of the earth's anger. Years of solid infrastructures were demolished in seconds. The sea advanced over the earth, covering entire cities. Despair became the oxygen that the whole nation breathed for the months that followed. In that context, this pastor told me how the Church was awakened in acts of love, bringing light in the midst of darkness. Pastors and ministers had died during the event. Hundreds of people were isolated and orphaned, and there were no leaders. For this reason, many teenagers and young people were sent to pastor congregations in that dramatic setting. God manifested Himself with power in the midst of the crisis, and many anonymous men and women who were in intimacy were activated for a key hour in the nation. In just one instant, everything changed, and a group of children of the wind was blown by the mouth of God to bring life in the midst of many dry bones.

Something similar happened in Chile. We have traveled a lot to this beloved nation and also collected hundreds of testimonies about the earthquake and tsunami that shook that country on February 27, 2010. In this platform of crisis and despair, hundreds of men and women took their spiritual lamps and lit the darkness of the nation. We have witnessed a glorious awakening of the churches in this beautiful country in these last times. Forecasters say it now seems like the earth is moaning. A scientist called these events as if the planet had birth pains. Some of this is mentioned in the Word of God:

"For the earnest expectation of the creation eagerly waits for the revealing of the sons of God...For we know that the whole creation groans and labors with birth pangs together until now."
Romans 8:19, 22, NKJV

There are many signs that are happening, sounding like a trumpet in order to awaken the children of God. The earth cries, the oceans roar, nations moan. Where are the children of God? There are hundreds of religious people in the world today. However, we need an army of sons and daughters who manifest the Father.

In my travels to the Middle East and Israel, I have noticed that the events taking place on that land announce how biblical and prophetic times are accurately fulfilled. Muslims have taken all geographical locations that the Word of God prophesies Jesus will occupy at His return. Satan and his army are responding to the biblical signs. (They seem to know the bible better than many Christians.) However, the earth continues to moan and cry out for the children of God. God will shake everything until the generation that God has set for this hour is fully awakened.[51] Just like a tsunami, a revival of the knowledge of His glory will fill the whole earth as the waters cover the sea.[52] Children will manifest the glory of the Father in all nations, and then the permanent Kingdom will be established. The earthquake infrastructure of the kingdom of darkness which has been built up for years will be reduced to nothing in divine instants. A generation of sons and daughters is being born, and they will prepare the way for the Beloved One to return and for His beauty to be seen by every eye. This is the hour of the revolution of the children of God.

True Worshipers are Children

Jesus announced that the end times would bring a multiplication of adulterated things. False apostles, prophets, worshipers, doctrines, deceiving spirits, and so forth. This has to do with the manifestation of the spirit of the antichrist that is among us, just as John has warned us.[53]

In that context, a generation of true ones must be raised up.

> *"But an hour is coming, and now is, when the true*
> *worshipers **will worship the Father** in spirit and truth;*
> *for such people the Father seeks to be His worshipers."*
> **John 4:23, NASB**
> Emphasis added by the author

I have heard this Scripture drawn from the dialogue between Jesus and the Samaritan woman hundreds of times. It is mentioned in every worship conference. There are excellent explanations of what it means to worship in spirit and in truth, about how the Father seeks for worshipers rather than worship, and many similar revelations. However, I have hardly heard about the relationship that Jesus makes between true worship and fatherhood. *"The true worshipers will worship the Father."* Why doesn't it say: God Almighty or Jehovah or the Messiah or the Holy One of Israel? It says: the Father. *True worshipers are children.* This is the time of the children. The generation the Father is seeking for are those to whom the Spirit of adoption has been revealed as we have seen throughout this book. God is not looking for children of religion. They are everywhere. However, if "He who sees everything" needs to be looking for true ones, it means that they are not easy to find. *The sons and daughters who live the nature of the Father and who cry Abba, they are the object of desire of God's heart.* For this dark hour that the earth is living now, there is no other option than the manifestation of the children of God. Worship and understanding of God's fatherhood are two sides of the same coin. The reason why there is often no true worship in the churches is because of the orphanhood that works within the people of God. The spirit of slavery produces fearful people who cannot confidently approach the arms of the Father. With thoughts of condemnation and corrupted motivations, children of religion make worship somewhat superficial and feigned. They do not understand that the sole desire of a father is to receive the spontaneous and pure love of his children. Jesus makes it clear, true worshipers worship the Father. "The Father" seeks sons and daughters. When passing His eyes of love across your heart, will He find a son or daughter of intimacy who is willing to give Him what He wants to receive and who will respond to the cry of the earth for this prophetic hour?

Enjoying and Being Enjoyed

When I return home after a ministerial trip, I just can't wait to have my daughter in my arms and give her a whole bunch of kisses. The Father's greatest desire is to enjoy us. A few days ago, after many hours of flight, I arrived at our apartment. As soon as I opened the door, a whirlwind called "Conie" was moving from side to side without stopping. She was so excited that Dad had returned home, and she ran, jumped, shouted and laughed without stopping. She brought me her toys and with her few words in baby-talk, it seemed like she wanted to sum up her activity of the last days in a matter of few seconds. I only wanted to hold her and enjoy her, but she would not sit still. When she was younger, she used to spend hours in my arms and sleeping on my chest. However, as we grow, we exchange the warmth of being enjoyed by the Father for hundreds of activities. I love watching my daughter play and run, but there is a moment when I just want to hug her and say things so deep to her that I cannot say while her rhythm is so hasty. At last, she finally surrendered in my arms and sank into my chest. For the next few minutes I could enjoy her and I felt that she enjoyed me. I began to tell her words that can only be expressed in intimacy: *Daughter of mine, I love you so much. In the last few days I could not stop thinking about you even for a minute. I believe in you so much. I know that you will be a woman who will reach farther than your parents, you will go to more nations, and you will run faster. Dad delights in you, you give him pleasure and I love to enjoy you every day.*

The Father Is Looking for Children to Enjoy and Who Enjoy Him

In that connection of love, God wants to reveal His deep secrets as to His expectations and purposes for His children. However, we are so full of occupations and ministerial obligations, labor, and all kinds of busyness. Sometimes I have to wait for my daughter to fall asleep so I then can speak to her and express my heart in depth. Does God have to wait for us? The Father is searching—looking for those who yearn to rest in His arms and fall into His bosom. Every morning He wants to enjoy you. *Intimacy with God is to enjoy Him and be enjoyed by the Father.* This is the generation that is being born in intimacy. In that bond of love without fear, the children of God will be nourished and strengthened to fulfill the task that this hour demands. The worshipers whom the Father is seeking, those who worship Him in spirit and in truth, they are far more than singers and musicians. They are sons and daughters who want to live in intimacy with the Father and who want to do His will at all times. They are those who only do what they see the Father doing, and say what they hear Him saying. They have overcome orphanhood and religiosity. Activity and daily running do not get them distracted from the Father's wishes. They operate from a place of love and from their restored identities. Those who have been redefined by Heaven are the ones who will become the answer to the cry of the earth in the end times.

Spirit of Abortion

The sons and daughters who have authority, received in intimacy, are the main characters of the greatest revolution for the coming seasons. Wherever there is one of them, there will be open heavens, in universities, squares, and shopping malls. Wherever a beloved child is found, the Father's voice will be heard on earth and the Spirit will descend with power. Some of the clearest signs that this is the time for the children are the murky attempts—in hundreds of governments— to legalize abortion. In the Bible, every time the government legalized abortion, it was the prelude that a child who was to be liberator for the nation was about to be born or had just been born. Shortly before Moses' birth, Pharaoh "promoted a law" for midwives to kill the unborn males. As they say on TV: "Any resemblance to real persons or events is purely coincidental." We all know the story: that basket on the river was the divine Grace that was protecting this liberator. Much later in the biblical story, Jesus, the "Son and liberator" had just been born. Herod proclaimed an edict for all male babies to be killed. Joseph took Jesus to Egypt and, in this way, God preserved His life for His prophetic destiny. It is very interesting that every time governments, kings, presidents or legislative chambers promote the legalization of abortion in nations, or attacks against children, liberators of nations are being born. These Machiavellian satanic plans are the response of the kingdom of darkness to what God is sending upon earth. We must rise up with authority against all these movements as never before, with the full understanding that Satan will not be able to abort a generation of liberators, sons and daughters who will take action bringing freedom to the nations. All these acts of corruption have a limit, says the Bible, and it has to do with the revolution of the children of God:

> *"The creation itself also will be delivered from the bondage of corruption into the glorious liberty of the children of God."*
>
> **Romans 8:21, NKJV**

Although the full and absolute fulfillment of these words from Paul to the Romans will take shape at the return of Christ, the Millennium, and the establishment of His Kingdom permanently, we must begin to live a dimension of all these truths today. The Kingdom is coming, but according to Jesus, the Kingdom is also here and now. If it were not so, Jesus would not have taught His disciples to pray, *"Your kingdom come. Your will be done on earth as it is in heaven."*[54] The "here and now" are the sons and daughters of intimacy who will manifest the freedom from Heaven in every place. The curse we see in the nations is the prelude to a great revival and a powerful manifestation of the glory of God. The closer it comes to its end, the government of Satan attempts to perform desperate acts of cursing in order to bring fear to the people of God. He's burning his last ammunitions. The wars in the Middle East, massacres, tragedies, catastrophes, and epidemics, will not be able to stop a generation of children who have their eyes fixed on the Father, who act in faith, and who wait for the fulfillment of the latter glory.

Seeing What the Father Is Doing

The earth cries out for the manifestation of the children of God. The Father seeks worshipers: sons and daughters who live in intimacy. The enemy tries to kill the children. As you will see, being a child of intimacy positions you in the center of the scene. When you are restored to your eternal identity, you become the answer to the cry of the earth, the object of desire and delight of the Father, and also a target for the kingdom of darkness. But do not be afraid, *God continues to use grace baskets to protect those children who will become liberators.* John reveals to us one of Jesus' most powerful secrets to exercise His ministry. In the Bible, this Scripture that I share below bears the title of "The Authority of the Son" (note the link between being a son and having authority in those words).

> *"Jesus gave them this answer: «Very truly I tell you, the Son can do nothing by Himself; He can do only what He*

> *sees His Father doing, because whatever the Father does
> the Son also does. For the Father loves the Son and shows
> Him all He does. Yes, and He will show Him even greater
> works than these, so that you will be amazed.»"*
>
> **John 5:19-20, NIV**

Jesus operates with authority from *"what He sees His Father doing."* The source that nourishes His ministry is that He has His eyes fixed on what His intimate Creator is doing on earth. When asked why He healed a man on the "Sabbath" day, He answered, *"My Father is working until now, and I Myself am working."*[55] *Intimacy brings law to life, though law always wants to kill intimacy.* Watching what the Father does, strengthens you. Operating from what Satan accomplishes, weakens you. Many Christians simply respond to what Satan does in a reactive way. This positions them a step behind the enemy. God is always one step ahead. There is nothing more powerful than undoing the works of the devil while you are being guided by what the Father is doing, and thus, establishing His works. The Bible anticipates everything the enemy is developing and reveals to us God's response for each circumstance. God did not call us to make *"piquetes"* (an Argentine expression for social or political manifestation in claim to something) or strikes against the kingdom of darkness. He said that those who have revelation from the Father are a rock, and that the gates of hell will not prevail against the Church.[56] So Satan is the one who will try to make manifestations or *piquetes* against the children of God who arise and advance, but he cannot contain the assaults of the sons and daughters of Light who will overcome the darkness. The secret of the authority that the children of God need in this dramatic hour lies in keeping a firm eye on Abba's movements. As long as you observe what Satan is doing, you will be weakened. In all areas, there is something that God is doing and something the devil does. What are you focusing on? For example, if I concentrate on what the enemy is trying to bring against my family, I become weak. There will be attacks, mistakes, and slips. But, if I begin to see what God is doing in my household, I strengthen myself to be able to transform the adversities. The same thing happens with the Church. I travel through many nations watching the work of God in various areas. I can clearly see that Satan is trying to corrupt and pollute, and he is succeeding in many places. But, I also see that God is moving with power and operating greatly in the Church. If I focus on the former, I weaken, but the power to overcome the enemy lies in fixing my eyes on what the Father is doing. The same thing happens in a nation, and in all the nations. Newscasts are the expression of what the darkness is doing on earth. There are people who spend more time watching or reading the news than praying and reading the Bible—the newspaper from Heaven. That is why they are weak when it comes to undoing the deeds of evil. The greatest source of authority and power lies in the intimacy with the Father. Despite Lucifer's desperate attempts to make us believe that God has lost control and that He has retired to a distant island in the beyond, having revelation in God's movements on earth is the key to being part of the revival that is about to be manifested in the nations.

There are things that God is conceiving, and there are other things that, by His infinite sovereignty and wisdom, are not happening. What are you focusing on? When John the Baptist saw Jesus for the first time, he declared, *"Behold! The Lamb of God who takes away the sin of the world!"*[57] He described to his followers that this man he was about to baptize was the One whom he had been preaching and speaking of, the Messiah who everyone expected and needed. However, when the excitement of Jesus' baptismal service had left, it seems that the greatest of the prophets was unfocused. In Luke chapter 7, the scenario is different. John was in prison and doubt invaded him. He failed to see what the Father was doing and instead he focused on what was not happening. Days went by and he was not released from jail. He heard a couple of jailers talking to each other about the rumor that Herod's wife would beg for his head. Then John sent his messengers to ask Jesus, *"Are You the Expected One, or do we look for someone else?"* You can see the blur in the question. How is this possible? A few days before this man had an absolute conviction that Jesus had been the provision of the Father for a lost people. Now, he just changed the perspective. Circumstances, the day's news, and hallway rumors have weakened him. Jesus' answer is profound. He does not take the easy way to say: Yes, I am. He chooses to re-focus on what is happening. *"Go and report to John what you have seen and heard: the blind receive sight, the lame walk, the lepers are cleansed, and the deaf hear, the dead are raised up, the poor have the gospel preached to them."*[58] In other words He is saying, *John, look no longer to what Satan is doing. He has put you in jail and he wants to behead you. Instead, focus on what the Father is doing. There are fabulous things that are happening, can you see them?*

Only a child who has been on the Father's lap can have this perspective. He would trust Dad in spite of the circumstances. There are dramatic events happening on earth today. Does this mean that Satan has more and more power? Or is this a sign that every word of God is being fulfilled, and that a trumpet is sounding for the children of God to come to the stage of the nations? Are you focused on what God is doing or on what the enemy is doing? Do you feel strong or weak to operate on the purpose that this time requires?

In recent years, I have clearly observed in all nations a generation that is entering into intimacy. They are being restored in their identity as intimate sons and daughters. They not only do works for God, but they are also entering the place of divine delight and pleasure with the Father. In that place, they are being trained, revitalized, nourished, and sent to the nations like arrows in the quiver of the Brave One. The Father is looking for them, the earth cries for them, and hell asks for their heads. This is a key time for humanity. The veil is falling from the eyes of many children of religion. God is shaking the rigid structures. The newspaper of Heaven announces a revival that is coming to the earth. On the cover page you can read the headline: "The revolution of the children of God is approaching." They are the *Sons and Daughters of Intimacy*, the generation of those who will manifest God on earth.

PRACTICAL GUIDE CHAPTER 12

· *The Revolution of the Children of God* ·

Questions to share in groups, cells or leadership teams:

1. What are the signs in the world that reflect the cry of creation for the manifestation of the children of God?

2. What are the characteristics of God's children that should be seen and expressed in every city and nation?

3. What is Satan's strategy to try to spiritually abort the children of intimacy?

4. How can we manifest the Kingdom of God in our city?

Personal application exercise:

What circumstances has Satan used to try to destroy your life, but that God has redeemed as a testimony that will transform hundreds of people? Write below your experience when reading this book and being transformed into a child of intimacy. Tell your testimony to everyone you meet, publish it on social networks and make it public everywhere. Let everyone know that a new son/daughter of intimacy is ready to manifest the fatherhood of God on earth.

____

____

____

CONCLUSION

CONCLUSION

In these pages, we have traveled a path full of stories, teachings, deep words, and transforming experiences. In this same way, I imagine the young people of Galilee walking along with Jesus. In that process, with a discipleship of paternity, Jesus Christ removed every tumor of orphanhood from their hearts. He consumed their fears and revealed to them a pure love that was impossible to resist. They were so affected, and decided to live their lives to express to others what they had received. In this way, through their passion and intimacy with the Father, and filled with the Holy Spirit, they gave birth to a glorious and powerful Church. They were so similar to the original that they began calling them "Christians," in other words "little Christs." But, what happened to that generation of children of intimacy with the Father? What was it that has adulterated this divine essence in these last centuries? Returning to the former love is not a call to retreat, but to cultivate an intimacy with God as it was in the first days in order to take the next step.

In this book, we have been able to hear a voice from Heaven over the Church of Christ of these days. A call to die to several religious works and to be re-born to what comes from the Spirit. We have traveled a path of healing and restorative love that can only be provoked when we discover the eternal voice behind temporal letters. How wonderful is that sound inside of us! It cannot be compared to any human voice. The sheep know how to hear the voice of the Good Shepherd and I believe that a person is not truly free until they hear the Father saying to them: *You are my beloved child, and you bring pleasure to my heart.* The best news is that every day of your life the Holy Spirit will continue to preach to you about what the Father feels for you. I think this is already happening right now. The chains of slavery have begun to undo themselves. I can hear the bonds breaking. A path of freedom has opened up. *You are no longer a slave, but a child.* And as you march firmly, hand on hand with the Father, you will begin to receive your inheritance. The things you thought you should earn by human effort are legally gifted to you because of His divine love. So, in that process of receiving abounding grace, you will only want to collaborate with the Father. You will want to be a part of His affairs. You will begin to sleep to the temporary things and be awakened to the eternal. When you thought that the best has already happened, He will invite you to the mount of revelation. More aspects of His nature will begin to be implanted in your life. He will attract you, captivate you. His Presence will become the greatest entertainment of your soul. You will feel amazed and ecstatic. Your hunger will increase, you will want more of His Word, more of His glory, more of His purposes. Suddenly, you will realize that you no longer live, but Christ has possessed you. Then, you will become a father or a mother to others.

He started giving you fish miraculously, but He did not leave you there. Now He will have turned you into a fisher of men. You will enter into the reality that Christ does not only want to do this in you, but through you. You will begin to disciple others in a paternal (or maternal) way. You will feel more attracted to souls than tasks.

I can see many orphans who will run to you at this stage. As Moses did with Joshua, Elijah with Elisha, Paul with Timothy, Jesus with the twelve, you will quickly discover the greater purpose for which God has prepared you: to be a father/mother of generations. For this to happen, you must begin by offering yourself to those around you. In a natural way you will be fulfilling the Great Commission: *"Go therefore and make disciples of all the nations."* One of the oldest roots of the word "disciple" is "one who is begotten." That is why all the men of God in the Bible saw their disciples as their children. Living as a son or daughter of intimacy, and as a father or mother of orphans, you will grow in remarkable dimensions. In a few years, you will achieve what decades of religion could not reach. When you least expect it, you will find yourself right there, in the middle of God's scene. His eternal script will be in progress and the most important moment of His work will be coming. Jesus will cleanse the earth from all that hinders the love of His chosen ones for Him. Do you know the best news ever? You will help Him move those water drums and, finally, we will reign together for eternity. Heavens will descend on the earth, and everything will be according to the design and style of the One who was, who is, and who will ever be.

Nicodemus is dead, but someone who will help fulfill the prophetic designs of the Father has been conceived. From now on, you will live only for others to see the Eternal Father through your life; first, to those around you and then, to the ends of the earth. Remember, intimacy is not a place to visit, but a home to live in. You should always go out and then return to that place. Do you feel like going out to show everyone who your Father is? Wait a moment. Before entering into action, you enter into intimacy. The Father of love has just opened the door, stop running for a moment. He is eagerly willing to enjoy you and He wants you to enjoy Him. Rest in His love. You haven't heard anything yet, He has many more things to tell you. Meanwhile, there is a feast in the Heavens, another child of the religion has just died, and a new *son or daughter of intimacy* has been born.

NOTES

CHAPTER 1
Sons and Daughters of Intimacy
1. Psalm 139:16
2. John 12:45
3. John 7:50-52
4. John 19:39-42

CHAPTER 2
Children of the Wind
5. Acts 2:15-16
6. Galatians 2:20

CHAPTER 3
Eyes Fixed on the Father
7. Nehemiah 8:10
8. 1 Thessalonians 5:19
9. 2 Corinthians 3:18
10. Colossians 2:3
11. Psalm 32:8
12. Philippians 1:6
13. Haggai 2:7

FUNDAMENTAL PILLARS:

Intimacy / Bible
Church / Character
Great Commission
Kingdom Culture
End Times

*"TRAINING GOD'S SONS AND
DAUGHTERS TO MANIFEST THE
ETERNAL KINGDOM IN THE NATIONS"*

TRAIN WITH US

—— Activate your purpose ——

Technical, theological, and practical training in an environment of worship, intimacy with God, communion with the Holy Spirit, and passion for Jesus. Our training options are as follows:

ATTENDANCE MODE

ONLINE MODE

ATTENDANCE MODE

LEADERSHIP CAREER
"Training leaders full of the Holy Spirit and passion for Jesus, who love and guide others to a destiny of glory"
(Three-year program. Attendance 1 or 2 days a week)

WORSHIP CAREER
"Training music ministers that, through music and worshipping, may lead the Church to experience God's Presence"
(Three-year program. Attendance 1 or 2 days a week)

AUDIOVISUAL AND MEDIA CAREER
"Training communicators from God's heart that manifest the designs of heavens on earth through digital art"
(Two year program, attendance once a week)

NEW GENERATION, CHILDREN'S CAREER
6 TO 11 YEARS OLD – *Online and attendance*
"Training children full of the Holy Spirit to be worshippers and intercessors in this generation"
(Two-year program, attendance and online, once a week)

EMERGING GENERATION, A CAREER FOR TEENAGERS
12 TO 17 YEARS OLD – *Online and attendance*
"Training teenagers that creatively manifest God's heart for this generation"
(Two-year program, attendance and online, once a week)

CLASSES STARTING IN MARCH AND AUGUST

ONLINE MODE ❯

MINISTERIAL CAREER

The purpose of the online ministerial career is to equip sons and daughters of God by providing them with tools that transform their inner self and encourage them to prepare others. Find out what your assignment is within God's eternal plan, and prepare the Church for the great day of Christ's return.

(Three-year program)
Classes starting in March and August

OTHER COURSES

Become a messenger of the Kingdom for your community! Enhance your intimacy with the Holy Spirit, become more passionate about the Scriptures, learn how to lead others to their destiny of glory, and grow in understanding and passion for Christ's return.

Do it through online courses or be part of our membership (getting access to all our courses available monthly), studying from home according to your availability.

- **Revelation:** The Revelation of Jesus in the End Times

- **Spiritual Leadership**

- **Restoring the Five Ministries in the Body of Christ**

- **Prophetic Ministry**

- **Experiences with the Holy Spirit**

- **Introduction to the End Times**

- **Leadership and Discipleship**

- **Character of the Kingdom**

For further information: www.misiononline.com

INTERNSHIP ❯

"Answering to the calling of God in a radical way"

Career focused on people who live outside of Buenos Aires and long to live the experience of setting aside to train in a context of passion for God, experiencing the culture of the Kingdom in a practical and intensive way. The goal of the program is for students to discover their specific ministry, activate their gifts and abilities, and become agents of transformation for their local Church, cities, and nations.

It is an exciting process, where each person is restored, ignited, activated, and sent out to fulfill God's purpose through his Church and in the nations.

The training includes: ministerial classes, devotionals of worship and fellowship with the Holy Spirit, spiritual disciplines (intercession, fasting, evangelism, compassion), involvement in the local Church and coexistence with other students from different cities and nations.

(Full time program. Three years)
Classes starting in March

For further information: **www.misioninstituto.com**

Intimacy and Worship Room

Worship and intercession 24hs.

Follow us live on YouTube:
/ MiSion CEM

MiSion Música

We are a family longing to manifest the eternal Kingdom of God
in the nations through prophetic music.

mision_musica

MiSion Música

MiSion Música

- OTHER PROGRAMS -
CONFERENCES AND ACTIVITIES

Intimacy with the Beloved

Intimacy with the Beloved is a congress of passionate worship that was born with the purpose of bringing the Church closer to the heart of God and knowing Him intimately.

- Month of July -

Jesús the Highest Pleasure

Two days of intimacy and passion for Jesus. For the Church of the end times, God is revealing the beauty and glory of Jesus in extraordinary ways.

- Month of February -

Immovable Generation

Live a week of intensive training, intimacy with Jesus and activation in the purpose of God for the nations and for the Church in this time.

- Month of February -

Find out about other activities by entering our website:
www.misioninstituto.com

OTHER BOOKS BY THE AUTHOR

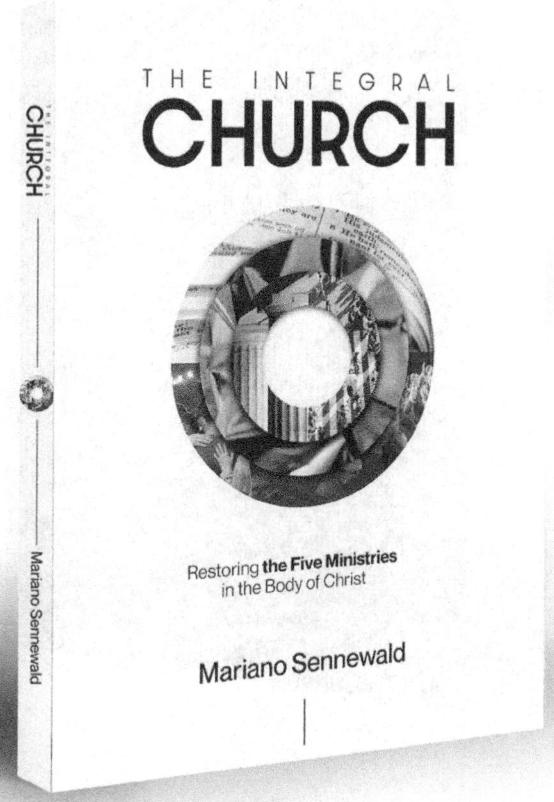

The Integral Church

God promised to perfect His Church until the day of Jesus Christ. To do so, He chose a design of five ministries that are intended to bring all the saints to the measure of the stature of Jesus. The purpose of the Gospel is not to fill the temples with people, but to fill the people with Christ. Discover these five characteristics of Jesus and how to develop these dynamics in your life through *"The Integral Church"*.

Also available in Spanish, in physical and digital format
www.misioninstituto.com/tienda-online

The Passions of the Heart of God

When you speak with someone, you will very soon recognize the things they are ardent about because they speak so fervently about them. If the Scriptures are an intimate dialogue with God, what are the topics He speaks about with irrepressible passion? What things are mentioned with overwhelming desire? Which ones does God name more often, and more emphatically? What does the Word say, specifically, about things that God loves? In this book you will discover seven areas God'd heart is passionate for. These longings will become the goal of your being, a guide to prayer and intercession, an action map, a ministry plan, the itinerary for your life's journey, a holy zeal to see others also shaping their hearts according to God's.

Also available in Spanish, in physical and digital format
www.misioninstituto.com/tienda-online

BOOKS IN SPANISH

Get our books at:

www.misioninstituto.com/tienda-online

CONTACT US

editorial@misioninstituto.com
www.misioninstituto.com
Benavidez 280 | Monte Grande
Buenos Aires, Argentina
+54 9 11 3090-3522

MISION / Centro de Entrenamiento

mision_instituto

MiSion CEM

Mariano Sennewald

mariano_sennewald

mgsennewald

Made in the USA
Las Vegas, NV
27 December 2024

15397187R00144